The Menopause Book

Books by Sheldon H. Cherry, M.D.

Understanding Pregnancy and Childbirth

The Menopause Myth

For Women of All Ages

Planning Ahead for Pregnancy

Medical, Surgical, and Gynecologic Complications of Pregnancy

The Menopause Book

A Guide to Health and Well-Being for Women After Forty

Sheldon H. Cherry, M.D., and Carolyn D. Runowicz, M.D.

Macmillan Publishing Company
New York

Maxwell Macmillan Canada
Toronto

Maxwell Macmillan International
New York   Oxford   Singapore   Sydney

Macmillan Publishing Company
866 Third Avenue
New York, NY 10022

Maxwell Macmillan Canada, Inc.
1200 Eglinton Avenue East, Suite 200
Don Mills, Ontario M3C 3N1

Macmillan Publishing Company is part of the Maxwell Communication Group of Companies.

Library of Congress Cataloging-in-Publication Data
Cherry, Sheldon H.
   The menopause book: a guide to health and well-being for women after forty /
Sheldon H. Cherry and Carolyn D. Runowicz.
      p.   cm.
   Includes index.
   ISBN 0-02-524758-1
   1. Menopause—Popular works.   I. Runowicz, Carolyn D.   II. Title.
RG186.C479   1994
618.1'75—dc20   93-21412

Macmillan books are available at special discounts for bulk purchases for sales promotions, premiums, fund-raising, or educational use. For details, contact:
         Special Sales Director
         Macmillan Publishing Company
         866 Third Avenue
         New York, NY 10022

10 9 8 7 6 5 4 3 2 1
Printed in the United States of America

To our patients

Contents

Contents

Acknowledgments

The authors would like to thank Lori Miller Kase for her help in editing the manuscript. Additional thanks to Ellen Levine, Natalie Chapman, Shelby Grayson, and Evelyn Tolliver.

We also thank Montefiore Medical Center for providing material for use in chapter 15.

Introduction

Women in the United States today can look forward to living an average of seventy-eight years, and their life expectancy continues to lengthen. In fact, women ages sixty-five and older make up the fastest-growing segment of our population. Their ranks, which now number over 15 million, are expected to approach 25 million by the turn of the century. Despite advances in longevity, the median age of menopause has remained constant at fifty-one years. Thus, postmenopausal women still have a full third of their lives left to live. This book is dedicated to that last third of a woman's life, the years after menopause.

The term *menopause* literally refers to the cessation of menstruation, though it is often used to describe the entire period surrounding this singular event. The transition from normal reproductive life to menopause—often referred to as the *climacteric*—begins at about age forty-five with a gradual decline in ovarian function, and lasts about five years. During this time, a woman may experience changes in her menstrual cycle, as well as other symptoms.

Unfortunately, superstition and misinformation have for too long characterized people's concept of—and reactions to—

this normal phase of life. In many women's minds, menopause is inextricably linked to infirmities and physiologic changes that herald the beginning of the end. They expect the "change of life" to bring with it multiple adverse feelings, depression, and rapid aging. Some worry that their husbands will no longer find them desirable, or that they will turn into the cranky and frustrated prototype of the "menopausal woman." These are some of the oldest myths to have plagued women.

Women's magazines, newspapers, and drug companies bombard both physicians and patients with conflicting information about menopause, and help to promulgate yet another myth about this natural stage of aging: that menopause is a deficiency disease requiring automatic treatment. Although opinions vary within the medical profession regarding care for the menopausal woman, we object to the notion that menopause is a disease. Many women are taking hormones that have not been proven safe or effective. While these drugs may be helpful for some women, they are not warranted in every case.

The purpose of this book is to expose the myths, both ancient and modern, surrounding menopause. By presenting facts based on medical research, we offer a true (and, we hope, reassuring) picture of what to expect from the change of life. You must not think of menopause as a turning point after which life goes downhill. Instead, it is a time to create new lifestyle patterns, which may or may not include hormone replacement, to ensure that the last third of your life is healthy and productive. Menopause is not the end of life, but the beginning of a new life—a time when unfulfilled ambitions can be realized and new freedom enjoyed.

The Menopause Book

1

Menopause:
A Historical Perspective

Renewed interest in menopause started in the 1960s. Until then, menopause had been something that women simply went through—and rarely talked about. Women who had complaints or problems were told to put up with them, that they would pass. Sometimes they were handed a prescription for Valium to help them "calm down." This seeming lack of compassion on the part of doctors stemmed from the fact that there was not much they could offer: there were no operations, no tests, and no wonder drugs. As long as menopause was a condition about which nothing could be done, the medical profession could ignore it.

The introduction of synthetic estrogen (Premarin) in the early 1960s changed all that. Hormone replacement therapy rapidly became a widely touted "treatment" for menopause— and menopausal women became a prime target for drug manufacturers. Some people wonder if the pharmaceutical industry turned menopause into a disease to create a market for new products.

In her book *The Menopause Industry*, Sandra Koney suggests that the pharmaceutical industry had a vested interest in medicine's discovery of the mid-life woman. Menopause-drug manufacturers, she says, created a "managed market" for a product with some potential benefits, but much potential harm. Synthetic estrogen, she believes, was developed before there was any clear indication for its use. The drug, therefore, was in need of a disease. Menopause fit the bill. After all, the baby boomers were heading toward midlife, and the greater the population with a disease, the greater the potential sales.

The use of tranquilizers in the pre-estrogen era paved the way for menopause's change in status from a normal biologic process to a treatable disease. At one time, symptoms such as boredom, anxiety, crying, and insomnia—all hallmarks of depression and anxiety—were attributed to menopause. (The emotional aspects of this stage of life will be addressed in chapter 4, but most of these psychological symptoms are no longer ascribed solely to menopause.) Advertising for tranquilizers helped shape the stereotype of the menopausal patient as overcome with depression and anxiety about aging. Drugs such as Valium and Seconal were said to help the menopausal woman to be serene— and no longer troublesome to her family.

The early work of Freud, which described menopause as a crisis period during which a woman mourned the end of her feminine attractiveness and childbearing capacity, did lend some credence to the notion of menopause as a mental illness. Indeed, to some psychiatrists, menopause spelled the loss of meaning in a woman's life. Terms such as "midlife crisis" and "empty nest syndrome" were used to explain the emotions women were supposed to suffer from at this time. Tranquilizers dulled these emotions and quelled anxiety; they provided a Band-Aid solution to the so-called problems of menopause.

Feminine Forever: The Rise of Estrogen

In the early 1960s, gynecologist Robert Wilson introduced the concept of "feminine forever": the "tragedy of menopause," he said, could be avoided by the use of estrogen "from puberty to grave." His epiphany coincided with the discovery of a cheap estrogen drug: Premarin. Once Premarin hit the market, tranquilizers were no longer necessary, because all of a woman's emotional complaints would now be abolished right along with her menopause, making her "feminine forever."

The drug companies, of course, supported Wilson's efforts to promote the use of estrogen. The media, too, touted Wilson's ideas, and organized medicine was forced to handle this. Barraged with requests from women patients, physicians began prescribing estrogen widely. Wilson and his cohorts described a huge range of serious "consequences" of estrogen depletion, including heart attack, stroke, brittle bones, dry and scaly skin, flabby breasts, and shrinking vagina. Lack of estrogen was also blamed for mood swings, depression, irritability, absent-mindedness, decreased libido, and even frigidity. Wilson frightened women with his bleak depiction of this "inevitable" decaying process.

Leading experts endorsed Wilson's views, and women by the millions took estrogen. Many physicians compared menopause to diabetes and thyroid disease. (Diabetes stems from lack of insulin; thyroid disease from underproduction of thyroid hormone.) We prescribe insulin and thyroid medication without hesitation if someone is deficient, they argued, so why not prescribe hormone replacement in menopause to avoid the multiple problems associated with estrogen deficiency?

The truth is, there is no proof that estrogen replacement therapy can accomplish all the miracles proclaimed by Wilson. It is not the elixir of youth, and it has been proven effective in alleviating only a limited number of conditions. Claims that hormones prevent aging-related changes in the hair, skin, and breasts are unsubstantiated. Still, exaggerated claims about estrogen remain commonplace.

Hormone Replacement: Risky Business?

Questions about the safety of estrogen therapy arose in the late 1970s, when several studies showed a distinct relationship between cancer of the uterus (specifically, of the uterine, or endometrial, lining) and the use of unopposed estrogen therapy in postmenopausal women. Sheldon H. Cherry, coauthor of this book, wrote a book called *The Menopause Myth* describing the danger. Postmenopausal women who were on estrogen experienced uterine cancer six to eight times more often than women who were not on estrogen, according to the studies. This dramatic finding caused great consternation among women. Was there a way, they wondered, to keep taking the "fountain of youth" pill while also avoiding cancer of the uterus?

Again, the drug companies came to the rescue. The drug progesterone (brand name Provera), which had been used to treat pregnancy disorders for many years, was added to the estrogen treatment. It is now known and accepted that the combination of estrogen and progesterone will prevent endometrial cancer. Although this particular problem was thus solved, many health advocates still question "treating" healthy women with any of these hormones.

Several studies have linked estrogen use to increased rates of breast cancer, though research in this area has yielded conflicting results. In addition, women's health advocates argue, these drugs are quite potent, and women are taking them for results that have not yet been proven. In fact, these drugs have not been around long enough for scientists to adequately evaluate the efficacy or safety of long-term use.

Hormones have been promoted as a cure for all the symptoms of menopause, yet many of the symptoms commonly associated with the change of life have little to do with menopause. If you consider only the problems definitely caused by estrogen loss, like hot flashes and vaginal dryness, the question of whether or not to take estrogen and progesterone for the rest of one's life—or at least for several years—takes on a very different meaning. To gain the proper perspective, we must identify which symptoms are hormonal, and then weigh the proven benefits of hormone therapy against the potential risks (see chapter 8).

Menopause as a Milestone

First of all, menopause has to be distinguished from the normal process of aging. Menopause itself is only one event in midlife. It is the last menstrual period. It does not last twenty years. Men go through midlife and experience many of the same "symptoms" that women do: depression, anxiety, skin changes, a decrease in sexuality, and other signs of aging. But there is no single event akin to the last period around which to focus these problems. The tendency is for menopause to get mixed up with—and blamed for—all the normal changes of midlife. Menopause focuses attention on the fact that a woman is getting older; it is the official confirmation of her passage into another stage of life.

Because our culture places so much value on youthful femininity, physical aging in women becomes linked to self-esteem and sexuality in a way that it does not in men. Reproductive ability is often confused with sexual ability, though the two are unrelated. For women, therefore, menopause becomes a symbol of decreasing sexual worth. Men, on the other hand, do not have this marker of the end of their reproductive capabilities, and they also continue reproducing longer than women.

Thirty years ago, the end of a woman's reproductive capability coincided with her declining worth to her family: as her children grew older and left the home, there was less for her to do. Things have changed. Careers are much more available and important to women in the nineties. Women now have more opportunities, and lead fuller lives. Menopause does not need to be the marker that it once was; it is just another milestone.

We do not want to diminish the significance of the problems some women experience at menopause. But whereas many menopausal women have difficult symptoms, others tend to blame all their midlife problems on menopause. Menopause is a convenient scapegoat: if problems are caused by the "change," they are out of a woman's hands.

The idea of menopause as a disease that causes multiple symptoms is a negative stereotype that lays the ground for unnecessary treatment—treatment that may, in the long run, do women more harm than good.

The Aging Process

Menopause does not produce aging. It is part of the aging process. Many of the problems associated in the past with menopause have more to do with the process of aging than with menopause itself. Aging occurs because of a gradual decline in the efficiency of organs. It is the opposite of the early phase of growth and development. Like other biological changes, the aging process is determined by heredity and physiology, and is influenced to some degree by the environment.

Aging is a complex process, and scientists have yet to determine precisely why it occurs. One hypothesis of aging, known as the theory of exhaustion, holds that a living cell has a fixed supply of energy, somewhat like a coiled spring. When the energy is used up, the coil unsprings, and life ends. The theory of genetic aging, on the other hand, holds that the hereditary factors in our cells (the genes) determine how long the cells will continue working. Ultimately, our life span is determined by how long our most important organs, such as the brain and heart, continue to function.

Aging does not affect the whole body uniformly, nor does everyone age in the same way. But in general, as one ages, one's body becomes less able to adapt to stress. While the young body can take a great deal of wear and tear before it begins to complain, the older body has lost a great deal of its resiliency.

The fear of aging has spawned a seemingly limitless market of youth-preserving products. Lotions and pills designed to forestall the inevitable are promoted extensively; nutrition experts hawk vitamins that promise miracles. In Romania, one physician injects her patients with a complex mixture of "rejuvenating" substances; another in Switzerland revitalizes his patients with living cells from the embryos of lambs. (These "medical miracles" are not available in the United States because they have failed to stand up to the scientific scrutiny required to determine their validity.)

This preoccupation with youth is nothing new. From the sorceress Medea, who brewed a potion of ram's blood, snake skin, and herbs to ward off aging, to Ponce de Leon, who crossed an ocean to search for the magical Fountain of Youth, humans have been looking for ways to preserve youth throughout history. Today people want to believe that hormone therapy can keep a woman young indefinitely. Unfortunately, this is simply not the case. We have tried various means of forestalling the aging process, and not one of them has been successful. Is estrogen any different?

Despite the widespread publicity, there is no evidence today that estrogen will alter the basic aging process or significantly extend the life span. It will not make a woman look younger, or even prevent wrinkles. It is not, and never can be, a panacea for all the problems of aging, and it certainly will not alleviate the emotional problems associated with middle age.

In the rest of this book, we try to separate the problems of menopause from the other problems of aging.

2
Hormones and the Female Reproductive Cycle

To truly understand menopause, you must familiarize yourself with the body's hormonal, or *endocrine*, system. A human being is a very complex creature. Performing functions like feeding, digesting, growing, and procreating requires good communication among the organs. One way that the various parts of your body communicate is via the nervous system, which comprises the brain, spinal cord, and nerves. This high-speed electrical system allows your body's central computer (brain) to talk to its various end terminals (organs).

An equally effective but slower conduit of information is the endocrine system. Certain organs send and receive chemical, rather than electrical, messages through the bloodstream. Their messengers are called *hormones*, a word derived from the Greek word *hormon* (to stimulate or excite). These chemicals maintain the balance of human life.

A hormone is any substance produced by a gland in one part of the body that produces an effect in another part of the body (see figure 1). The pituitary gland at the base of the brain, for example, secretes many hormones: one, human growth hormone, affects the body's skeletal system and determines stature; another, follicle-stimulating hormone (FSH), sets the menstrual cycle in motion. The adrenal glands unleash cortisone and adrenaline, which enable one to stand up to the acute stresses of life. And ovaries produce estrogen and progesterone, which help to establish and maintain a pregnancy.

The complex interplay between the body and its hormones is evident in the way the body handles stress. During the "fight or flight" reaction, which evolved when our ancestors encoun-

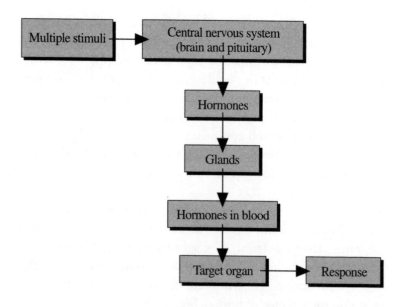

FIGURE 1 *In response to various stimuli (e.g., fear or stress), the central nervous system produces hormones, which serve as messengers. They are carried to glands, which in turn secrete hormones (e.g., adrenaline) that travel through the bloodstream to a target organ, where the response to the stimulus (e.g., rapid heartbeat) is triggered.*

tered danger and had to either flee or fight for their lives, the body undergoes swift changes. The heart beats faster. Blood and oxygen surge to the muscles and brain. All of this starts with perception of a stressor in the brain and ends with the release of hormones from the adrenal glands.

Hormones govern virtually every aspect of human experience, from growth and development to reproduction and me-

TABLE 1
Female Hormones

HORMONE	SITE OF PRODUCTION	FUNCTION
Thyroid hormones	Thyroid gland	Heat regulation Growth Metabolism Energy
Insulin	Pancreas	Food metabolism
Gonadotropin hormones (FSH, LH)	Pituitary gland	Sexual and reproductive function
Estrogen and progesterone	Ovaries	Sexual and reproductive function
Parathyroid hormone	Parathyroid gland	Bone metabolism
Cortisone	Adrenal glands	Stress maintenance Basic metabolism
Growth hormone	Pituitary gland	Growth, maturation, and metabolism

tabolism. They control the processes necessary to meet the energy and growth needs of the body. They generally maintain the internal milieu. Table 1 illustrates the complexity and abundance of hormones in the female system.

Female sexual and reproductive functions depend on hormones. The sudden flow of sex hormones into the bloodstream produces puberty and menstruation (and, alas, acne). The delicate interplay of these and other hormones prepares the female body each month for pregnancy. Much of how women function, as well as how they age, involves the reproductive hormones. The presence of these hormones is integral to a woman's menstrual cycle; their absence explains many of the changes that occur at menopause.

Estrogen, in particular, affects the body in many ways as its level varies throughout the life cycle (see figure 2). It causes the reproductive and genital organs to mature; conversely, its absence causes these organs to shrink, or atrophy. Estrogen is also involved in bone metabolism; lack of estrogen can lead to porous bones (see chapter 7 on osteoporosis). Estrogen helps keep skin elastic; estrogen deficiency leads to thinness and drying of the skin in the genital region. Estrogen also appears to protect premenopausal women against heart disease; when estrogen levels decline, cardiovascular disease risk increases.

To comprehend what happens to a woman's body and its hormones at menopause, it is important to understand the role that these hormones play before and during the reproductive years.

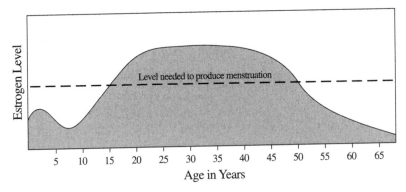

FIGURE 2 *Level of estrogen at five-year age increments. (Note: Estrogen is present after menopause, though it is not sufficient to produce menstruation.)*

Menarche

Menarche, the onset of menstruation, is the culmination of a series of hormonal changes that have quietly been occurring for several years. Before the age of eight, only limited amounts of estrogen, the "female hormone," are secreted. In fact, a young girl also makes small amounts of the male hormone, testosterone. Gradually, however, the production of female hormones exceeds the output of male hormones, and a recognizable pattern of changes emerges.

When a girl is between the ages of ten and fourteen, her brain's pituitary gland begins to produce the hormones that are integral to female development. One, FSH, will play an important part in the reproductive cycle. Another, growth hormone, accelerates bodily growth, which in the first decade of life occurs slowly and constantly.

As the body continues to grow and mature, the pituitary produces more FSH, causing the ovary to begin making estrogen. Estrogen causes the development of female sex characteristics in an orderly manner: first, the breasts develop and pubic hair grows; then, menstruation begins and underarm (axillary) hair appears; and finally, the hips begin to broaden, producing the characteristic feminine shape.

Estrogen produces other changes as well. By closing the ends of the bones, estrogen stops skeletal growth. Generally, girls stop growing in height as menstruation begins. Estrogen also causes fat to be deposited in the lips of the vagina, or labia, making them plumper. Pubic hair becomes denser and coarser in texture. The clitoris enlarges and becomes sensitive. The vagina increases in size and thickness, and growth occurs in the uterus, fallopian tubes, and ovaries (see figure 3 depicting the female reproductive system). Finally, as the body, brain, and hormone-producing glands mature, menstruation begins.

The average age of menarche is twelve to fourteen years, but it varies widely. Heredity plays a role in the timing of menarche just as it does in menopause, though, as we discussed earlier, girls today are beginning their periods earlier in life than their mothers. It is likely that physical condition, diet, and psychological factors all influence the age at which menstruation starts. Interestingly, early maturity is common in societies where sexual promiscuity is customary. Also, for some reason, more girls begin their periods in the winter.

As the uterus and ovaries mature, the bleeding pattern becomes cyclical, and menstrual cycles begin. For a year or more after menarche, the interval between periods often varies widely. The second period may not appear for six months, or may occur after three weeks. The pattern is usually not set for three to four years after the initial onset of flow.

The menstrual cycle depends on the relationship and function of the various hormone-producing glands. In order for a woman to have a period, the following events must take place:

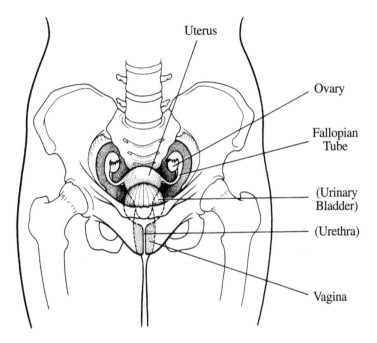

Uterus

Ovary

Fallopian
Tube

(Urinary
Bladder)

(Urethra)

Vagina

FIGURE 3 *The female reproductive system.*

1. The pituitary gland must receive signals from the brain to produce the hormone FSH.
2. The ovary must respond to this pituitary hormone by producing its basic hormones: first estrogen, and then, following ovulation, progesterone.
3. The uterus must react to the ovarian hormones. The lining of the uterus—the endometrium—first thickens, then regresses and bleeds, causing menstruation.

Any defect in this chain will result in not menstruating. This has bearing on our later discussion of menopause.

Estrogen, Progesterone, and the Menstrual Cycle

Estrogen is one of the two hormones produced by the mature ovary. The other is progesterone. The basic function of both hormones is to prepare the body for reproduction. Estrogen is responsible for producing an environment in the uterus suitable to receive a fertilized egg and produce a successful pregnancy. Progesterone ensures that the uterus is in the proper condition to support a pregnancy. However, progesterone will have no effect on the uterine lining unless the lining has been first prepared by estrogen stimulation. Progesterone alone will not produce a period.

On day one of the menstrual cycle (the day the period starts), the brain secretes FSH, which stimulates the ovaries to produce estrogen. As the level of estrogen rises, it inhibits the pituitary gland's production of FSH, and stimulates the formation of another pituitary hormone, luteinizing hormone (LH). LH causes the ovary to ovulate (ovulation usually occurs between days twelve and fifteen of the normal twenty-eight-day menstrual cycle) and stimulates the production of progesterone.

Estrogen and progesterone maintain the uterine lining in a state in which a fertilized egg can become lodged and obtain nutritional support. If pregnancy does not occur, the estrogen level falls, the endometrial lining of the uterus breaks down, and a period occurs. Just as high levels of estrogen suppress the release of FSH, low levels of estrogen trigger the pituitary gland to increase its production of FSH, and the cycle begins again. This process is an example of the reciprocal relationship between the ovary and the pituitary.

This physiological phenomenon underlies the mechanism of birth control pills. Oral contraceptives, which contain both estrogen and progesterone, prevent ovulation by inhibiting or limiting the production of FSH to quantities not sufficient to produce an ovulation cycle.

Menstruation and PMS

Menstruation is defined as any periodic bleeding from the endometrium (uterine lining), usually in a recurring pattern. The local tissue growth and blood vessel changes that lead to menstrual bleeding are a direct result of stimulation by the ovarian hormones, estrogen and progesterone. Menstruation is nature's way of dealing with the body's not becoming pregnant. The elaborate preparations for possible pregnancy are discarded in anticipation of the next cycle.

Most women believe that their periods occur at regular intervals—usually in twenty-eight-day cycles. However, if you were to keep an accurate record of your cycles, you would probably find that the intervals between your periods vary a day or two from month to month. As you age, your cycle tends to get shorter. Adolescent girls show the most variation in length of cycle, with an average interval of thirty-four days. Normal adult women have average cycles of twenty-four to thirty-two days. Menstrual flow lasts an average of four to five days, with a normal variation of two to eight days.

Unusually frequent periods—coming more often than every three weeks—may not be linked to ovulation. The same can be said of unusually infrequent periods that are uncharacteristically heavy. Bleeding from the uterus without ovulation is called *anovulatory* bleeding. This type of bleeding is more common around the time of menopause.

The amount of blood lost during a period varies from woman to woman, and depends on age, well-being, and psychological state, but the average woman loses from 2 to 10 ounces each month. The blood, of course, is mixed in with the endometrial cells that are being cast off; menstrual discharge is only about 75 percent blood. Its characteristic odor is due to the presence of bacteria in the blood.

The old scientific literature (and some of the lay literature) suggested that the menstrual flow was designed to help the body get rid of toxic substances. However, there is no evidence at this time of the presence of any noxious element in the menstrual flow, nor of the body's need to eliminate toxins via this route. A new theory proposed by Margie Profet of the University of California at Berkeley suggests that menstruation evolved as a mechanism for protecting the uterus and fallopian tubes against harmful organisms delivered by incoming sperm. According to this theory, menstruation is not a passive loss of unused uterine lining but an aggressive way to prevent infection by viruses and bacteria.

The body probably has a lower resistance to infection in the days prior to menstruation. Infections such as herpes simplex (a viral disease of the vulva) and vaginal warts (human papilloma virus) are more likely to strike at this time of the month; so are outbreaks of skin acne.

Most women get by during menstruation with minimal discomfort, whereas others experience lower abdominal discomfort and pressure in the legs and pelvic area. The progesterone produced during the second half of the menstrual cycle is thought to be responsible for the salt and fluid retention that leads to abdominal bloating in the days preceding menstruation. Emotional uneasiness is also common at this time: women often experience an increase in tension, moodiness, and irritability. These symptoms are collectively referred to as *premenstrual syndrome,* or *PMS*.

Some experts blame progesterone and the fluid retention it causes for some of the psychic tension. Research has also suggested that some alteration in the production of endorphins, chemicals produced in the brain that provide a pain-relieving effect, may also play a role. In fact, exercise, which triggers the release of endorphins, is one of the only "treatments" for PMS that has been shown to be consistently effective.

Nonetheless, a wide range of remedies has been promoted to alleviate PMS, including certain vitamins, hormones, and even tranquilizers. Some women find that simple dietary changes, such as reducing caffeine and salt intake, can reduce premenstrual discomfort.

3

Menopause Defined

The term *menopause* denotes the cessation of menstrual periods. However, the end of menstruation is only one of a train of symptoms that mark the gradual transition from the reproductive years to the postreproductive years. The word *climacteric*, which is derived from the Greek *klimacter*, meaning "rung of the ladder," more accurately describes the multiple changes that occur over a period of several years. When people use the word menopause, they are usually referring to the climacteric.

The climacteric is the counterpart of puberty. Just as the onset of the menstrual flow is one of many related manifestations of puberty, menopause, or loss of menstruation, is just one of the signs that a woman is passing into another stage of life.

The life of a woman may be divided into five phases: childhood, puberty, maturity, climacteric, and older age. The transition from maturity to older age occurs gradually, over a period of approximately fifteen years, usually between the ages of forty-five and sixty. The actual cessation of menstruation usually takes place between the ages of forty-eight and fifty-two, with an average of about fifty-one.

The Onset of Menopause

Both heredity and constitution help to determine the age of menopause. Obese women, for example, tend to undergo menopause later in life than thin women. There is a tendency, too, for a daughter to follow the menstrual pattern of her mother; this tendency appears, for example, in a rare group of women who experience menopause in their late thirties or early forties. In general, a woman today can expect to experience menopause later in life than her grandmother did. Interestingly, girls have also tended to begin menstruating earlier in life than their mothers did. Researchers have suggested that better nutrition and health, as well as improved medical care, have contributed to the lengthening of the reproductive years.

Scientists have investigated several other factors in relation to menopausal age, but only two consistently stand out: altitude and cigarette smoking. Women living at higher altitudes are consistently found to experience menopause earlier. Heavy smokers can also expect to hit menopause sooner than nonsmokers. On the other hand, there is no relationship between the timing of menarche and that of menopause. Nor does the number of children one has or the age at which one first engages in sexual activity affect when one ceases menstruating. Though research has failed to show a relationship between oral contraceptive use and menopausal age, the pill can mask the onset of menopause because it produces an artificial period.

Premature Menopause

Premature menopause, defined as the cessation of menstruation before age forty, is rare. In fact, many cases of so-called premature menopause have turned out to be 8-pound boys! When menopause does occur early, there is often a family history of premature menopause or other illnesses.

If you undergo an early menopause, it is particularly important that you be diagnosed early so that you can be evaluated for hormone replacement therapy as quickly as possible. Because women who experience early menopause tend to live for many years without the benefits of estrogen on bones and the cardiovascular system, they are at higher risk for both heart disease and the debilitating bone disease osteoporosis. Thus, most doctors recommend hormone replacement, which significantly reduces such risks, for these women (see chapter 8).

Premature menopause can be an emotionally painful experience if a woman has not yet finished having children. But thanks to new reproductive technologies, premature menopause does not have to mean a premature end to the reproductive years. With hormonal priming and donor eggs, postmenopausal women—particularly those under forty-five—may still be capable of carrying out a pregnancy.

Late Menopause

Late menopause, where menstruation continues past age fifty-three or fifty-four, also tends to be hereditary. (Women with diabetes often have late menopause.) Although it is common to have regular periods up to the age of fifty-two, only 5 percent of women reach menopause after fifty-three. If you are in your mid-fifties and have vaginal bleeding, you should not automatically assume that you are still menstruating. Vaginal bleeding may also be due to some abnormality of the uterus (see chapter 14). Some physicians feel that women who do have late menopause are at greater risk for uterine cancer. If you continue to have vaginal bleeding of any sort at age fifty-three or beyond, you should be followed closely by your doctor.

Surgical Menopause

The so-called surgical menopause is caused by removal of pre-menopausal ovaries. If only the uterus is removed during a hysterectomy, ovarian function continues until the normal age of menopause, and cessation of the menstrual period is the only menopauselike symptom a woman immediately experiences. Even the surgical removal of one ovary does not affect ovarian function. But removal of both ovaries from a woman who is still menstruating causes the onset of severe symptoms in at least 50 percent of cases. A surgical menopause is more troubling than a natural one, because ovarian function terminates suddenly. If untreated, symptoms such as hot flashes and painful intercourse (caused by vaginal drying and thinning) can continue from months to years, and are more frequent and more severe than in natural menopause. However, these symptoms, which we discuss further in chapter 4, can be treated quite adequately.

Artificial Menopause

Radiation to the ovaries also can affect ovarian function, producing an artificial menopause and causing the same type of symptoms as surgical menopause. This occasionally happens when X rays are used to treat malignancies in the lower pelvic area. Certain types of chemotherapy also can produce artificial menopause, because these agents affect actively growing and dividing eggs. The effect of chemotherapy varies with the age at treatment, as well as with the dose and type of treatment. Artificial menopause caused by chemotherapy usually reverses after cessation of treatment.

Diagnosing Menopause

Because many women experience some irregularity in the length of their menstrual cycles before the onset of menopause, it is difficult to identify the last episode of menstrual bleeding when it occurs. In retrospect, of course, it is easy. In general, the older you are and the longer the duration between your periods, the more likely it is that you are approaching menopause. However, some women get more frequent periods just before menopause.

One way that your doctor can make a definitive diagnosis of menopause is by measuring follicle-stimulating hormone (FSH) levels in your bloodstream. With menopause, the ovary loses its ability to respond to FSH, so the brain continues to produce the hormone, and FSH levels in the bloodstream rise. Levels over 40 MIU/ml are commonly associated with menopause (FSH is measured in standard international units per milliliter of blood serum).

Cause of Menopause

Simply stated, the cause of menopause is ovarian shutdown. The ovaries stop ovulating, and cease to produce the hormones estrogen and progesterone, both of which, as you have seen, are vital to the reproductive cycle.

Between the onset of menstruation and menopause, the average woman undergoes about 400 ovulatory cycles—that is, she produces an average of 400 eggs that can potentially be fertilized. This is actually a very small percentage of the eggs present at birth. A woman is born with between 400,000 and 700,000 immature eggs in her ovaries. The vast number of these eggs degenerate, so that little over half remain at the onset of puberty. During each ovulatory cycle, usually only one of several immature eggs goes through a full growth cycle and on to ovulation; the rest regress, or become reabsorbed by the body.

Basically, menopause is an accentuation of this regression, rather than a depletion of the egg supply due to repeated ovulation. At menopause, the follicle cells surrounding the few remaining eggs can no longer respond to FSH; thus, the ovaries cease to produce viable eggs, and they eventually stop making estrogen and progesterone. But as we have discussed, the end of ovarian functioning does not happen overnight. There is a slow decline over a period of years, which causes characteristic symptoms (see chapter 4).

Even when the process of ovulation stops, periods may continue (anovulatory periods). Eventually, the periods become less frequent and cease. However, the production of estrogen may continue. There is laboratory and clinical evidence that the ovary may continue to secrete estrogen in variable amounts for some time after the actual end of the menstrual cycle, though not enough to cause menstrual flow. The fact that estrogen production declines at different rates may account for the variability in symptoms among women (see figure 4). In general, the more rapidly estrogen is depleted, the more intense menopausal symptoms will be.

What causes the ovary to gradually stop functioning altogether? Researchers do not know for sure, but they suspect some factor in the ovary itself is responsible. As noted earlier, the pituitary gland continues to produce FSH in an attempt to force the ovary to make estrogen. Since the ovaries fail to respond to the FSH by producing estrogen, very large amounts of FSH appear in the bloodstream; there is not sufficient estrogen to signal the pituitary to stop producing FSH.

Laboratory diagnosis of menopause is made not by the lack of estrogen, but, as we described earlier, by the large amounts of FSH present in the blood. This excess hormone may be respon-

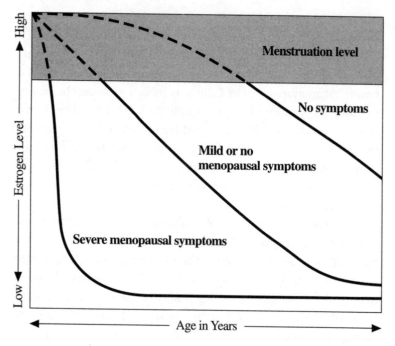

FIGURE 4 *Estrogen level falls as ovarian function decreases with age.*
The existence and severity of symptoms of menopause depend on the
rate of the fall of estrogen level.

sible for some of the symptoms characteristic of menopause. In
fact, some experts attribute all menopausal symptoms to an excess of pituitary hormones.

Though postmenopausal women have significantly lower
levels of estrogen than premenopausal women, studies have found
that most women continue to have some estrogen circulating in
their bloodstream after menopause. Even women whose ovaries
have been surgically removed often have estrogen in their blood.
Examination of the labia and vaginas of these women reveals a
wide range of estrogenic effects and an absence of vaginal atro-

phy. If the ovaries have stopped producing estrogen, what is the source of this hormone?

The major circulating hormone in postmenopausal women is an estrogen called *estrone*. In fact, it may be present in greater quantity in some postmenopausal women than it is in some pre-menopausal women. The adrenal glands, which are next to the kidneys, produce a hormone called *androstenedione*, which is converted to estrone by certain tissues in the body. Fat cells are particularly adept at this conversion. Women who are overweight, and therefore have more adipose (fatty) tissue, seem to produce more estrone.

A group of Texas doctors has shown recently that there is a site other than the adrenal glands and ovaries that produces estrogens in postmenopausal women, though they have not been able to pinpoint the exact source. These scientists have even noted an increase in estrogen production in some postmenopausal women. The adrenal glands and other tissues in the body may produce estrogens for many years. This continued presence of estrogen may account for the fact that many women experience very few menopausal symptoms.

4
Changes and Feelings at Menopause

What can you expect to experience at menopause? Many physical and emotional changes have been attributed to menopause by women, the media, and physicians. It is a convenient catchall diagnosis. But the truth is that there are only a few symptoms that are uniquely characteristic of the menopausal phase.

The Symptoms of Menopause

Hot flashes and painful intercourse (due to vaginal atrophy) are the most common symptoms. In fact, they are the only manifestations of menopause that are consistently relieved by estrogen replacement therapy, and can therefore be "blamed" on a deficiency in the hormone. There are a wide array of other possible symptoms (some that precede menopause and others that follow it), but their treatment is much less predictable.

Irregular menstruation will probably be the first sign that you are approaching menopause. In fact, 20 percent of women experience no other symptoms. During the climacteric, your periods may become further and further apart, eventually stopping completely. It is impossible for you to know which is your last period; only time will tell. Once the interval between periods lengthens to six months, it is likely that your menstrual cycle will soon cease. Once it does, pregnancy becomes impossible, and birth control can be stopped. To be cautious, however, some physicians recommend using birth control for up to one year after the last period—you never can be sure that it is your last until some time has elapsed.

After irregular menstruation, hot flashes are the most common—and troublesome—symptom of the climacteric. They may precede, by years or months, the actual menopause. Hot flashes are characterized by a sensation of intense heat in the upper part of the body, accompanied by a rising flushing of the chest, neck, and face, and are often followed by heavy sweating. The skin flush is not always visible, though some women may blush a deep red during the episode. The duration of the flashes varies between thirty seconds and about five minutes, with an average duration of four minutes. These flashes occur at irregular times during the day and night. Sometimes they are severe enough to interfere with your normal life pattern, resulting in insomnia or an increase in tension. (Waking in the middle of the night may be caused by the hot flash, or the hot flash may follow some other disturbance that awakens you.)

About 60 percent of women get hot flashes or other vasomotor symptoms such as dizziness and heart palpitations. (The term *vasomotor* describes bodily changes related to the constriction and dilation of the blood vessels.) These symptoms often decrease in strength and frequency with time, unlike symptoms such as vaginal dryness that get worse as the estrogen supply dwindles. Only 25 to 50 percent of those women who suffer from hot flashes will still have them after two years.

Hormone replacement treatment has been shown to be quite effective in reducing hot flashes, though the risks involved with hormone therapy must be weighed against this benefit. Sometimes hot flashes can be alleviated by simple measures like taking a cold shower, washing your face with cold water, or moving into a cool room.

Less common vasomotor symptoms include numbness and tingling in the hands and feet, heart palpitations, dizziness, and even fainting. We don't yet know what causes hot flashes and these related symptoms, though we suspect they are associated somehow to the depletion of estrogen and the subsequent twentyfold increase in FSH.

Interestingly, despite the fact that the hormone changes that occur at menopause are permanent, these kinds of symptoms are temporary. As we saw in figure 4, the rate at which estrogen levels decline may be related to the degree of symptoms. In fact, menopausal symptoms tend to be most severe in cases of surgical menopause, when estrogen falls rapidly. Hot flashes also occur when there is a sudden discontinuation of estrogen treatment. Even men treated with estrogens for prostate cancer complain of hot flashes after the medication is discontinued.

Other menopausal symptoms are more variable, and may take years to develop. Both genetic factors and the amount of estrogen being produced by tissues other than the ovaries come into play. Gradually, a woman's labia become thinner, less elastic, and less fatty. The vagina, too, may become drier and less elastic, a condition called vaginal atrophy. This change may produce some difficulty and discomfort with sexual intercourse. (See chapter 5 for more on sexuality after menopause.) The uterus and cervix shrink as well, but this has no clinical significance.

Hair may also become somewhat thinner over time, and a slight growth of hair may appear on the upper lip and chin. The breasts may lose some elasticity and fullness after menopause. Fat deposition in the body changes, and there may be an increase in the size of the buttocks and hips. Postmenopausal women have a tendency to gain weight, but this may be due to changes in thyroid gland function, as well as decreased physical activity and increased food intake. Some postmenopausal women complain of more frequent headaches, especially the migraine type; this may be associated with insomnia. But these problems do not necessarily stem from hormonal changes. Many of these symptoms are difficult to link to menopause; they can also be related to nervous tension and anxiety, which can be present at any time in life.

Which Symptoms Should You Expect?

Many of the symptoms just described are gradual in onset—if they occur at all. Old wives' tales have tended to worsen expectations. Fear of a natural process has interfered with our understanding of menopause, leading many women to expect a bleak period of sudden change, loss of beauty, immediate aging, and a sexless existence, all of which are far from the truth. The majority of healthy and well-adjusted women will pass through this period with a minimum of distress, and no more than 20 percent will require medical treatment for their symptoms. Actually, some women even look forward to menopause, since they no longer have to fear pregnancy or experience menstrual discomfort. Remember, menopause is a natural physiologic process and not a disease. If you suffer from severe symptoms, however, hormone therapy (or an alternative) is available and should be taken advantage of. We discuss these therapies in detail in chapters 8 through 10.

5

Emotional and Sexual Aspects of Menopause

Menopause was once viewed as the beginning of inevitable sexual and emotional decline in a woman's life. But now, as women are living longer and staying healthier, researchers are proving that, in fact, the opposite may be true. That menopause always leads to depression and decreased sexual desire is a longstanding misconception. There is little scientific literature to support either of these widely held beliefs. Not only do many postmenopausal women enjoy active and fulfilling sex lives, but studies have shown that they are less likely than premenopausal women to suffer from major depression.

Still, there are many differences of opinion regarding the relationship between menopause and the psyche. Some psychiatrists and gynecologists maintain that estrogen deficiency causes many psychological ills, whereas others insist that the only true symptoms of menopause are those discussed in chapter 4—cessation of menstruation, hot flashes, and vaginal dryness.

Psychological symptoms that have been attributed to menopause include not only depression and sexual dysfunction, but also decreased energy and drive, inability to concentrate, irritability, aggressiveness, anxiety, headaches, insomnia, nervous exhaustion, and mood swings. As you can see, these symptoms are quite varied and rather nonspecific. All can occur at any age, in men or women. Several of these symptoms are also associated with major psychiatric disorders—particularly depression and anxiety disorders—that sometimes reveal themselves around the time of menopause.

Psychiatric Illnesses

If you are middle-aged, you may be inclined to write off feelings of depression and anxiety as "menopausal." But both these symptoms can stem from underlying psychiatric illnesses. It is important, for example, to differentiate between a minor depressive mood, which will pass without intervention, and clinical depression, which can be much more serious. Similarly, anxiety that is severe enough to interfere with your day-to-day life is not the same as mild apprehension about an impending event.

Depression

Many of the complaints associated with depressive disorders suggest physical illness: in addition to mood changes, a depressed person may experience fatigue, decreased appetite, diminished energy, weight loss, constipation, headaches, difficulty in breathing, and unusual sensations in the chest, abdomen, and head. Feelings of sadness, loss of concentration, and even thoughts of death may occur. Though women of any age tend to be more susceptible to depression than men, researchers have failed to find an increase in depressive symptoms among middle-aged women. In fact, a number of recent studies have found that women ages forty-five to sixty-four actually had a significantly lower incidence of depression than women in other age groups. Still, if you suffer from at least three of the symptoms listed at the beginning of this paragraph, you may need to undergo counseling and perhaps a trial of an antidepressant medication such as Prozac.

Anxiety Disorder

Also more common in women than men, anxiety disorder is characterized by severe anxiety with underlying feelings of fear and apprehension. Other symptoms include tension and restlessness, sometimes associated with a dry mouth, sweating, headaches, palpitations, diarrhea, and difficulty in breathing. Such symptoms may also be caused by certain physical disorders, such as an overactive thyroid or hypoglycemia, so it is important that you be evaluated by a physician if you experience these symptoms.

Emotional Change and Menopause

Although they certainly do not corner the market on psychiatric illness, menopausal women do appear to have more minor psychological complaints than do women in other age groups. The hormonal changes associated with menopause may be sufficient to trigger some emotional problems. But feelings like depression and apprehension may also be related to events that are common in midlife: divorce, death of a spouse or parent, empty nest syndrome, or midcareer crises.

There appear to be many different variables that influence a woman's emotional experience at menopause:

- The meaning of menopause within her particular culture
- Her social class
- Whether or not she works outside the home

- The number of friends she has, and the nature of her social network
- The degree of her involvement with her children
- The occurrence of stressful life events such as divorce or death of a loved one
- The loss of her mother at an early age, which seems to be a particular event affecting midlife feelings
- Past history of depression, which may make her more vulnerable to emotional problems at this stage of life

Can medical professionals treat the emotional problems that arise at this time of life? Though some of these complaints are fleeting, they should not automatically be dismissed as part of menopause. You should discuss any questions about sexual function or changes in moods with your physician. Your psychological symptoms should be evaluated and treated appropriately, just as physical symptoms would be. Even a trial of hormonal therapy may be indicated. If you are experiencing symptoms of severe depression or any other psychiatric illness, you should be evaluated by the appropriate experts, just as you would be at any age.

Sexual Issues at Menopause

It has gradually been accepted that sexual activity does—and should—continue in older men and women, and, in most cases, is a desired and enjoyed form of communication and pleasure. Alfred Kinsey and his colleagues were the first to publish an extensive survey of sexual behavior in middle-aged and older women. They found that postmenopausal women retained sexual capacity, sexual interest, and the ability to achieve satisfaction. In fact, some women found sex more pleasurable, because they no longer feared pregnancy. The researchers concluded that there is no age limit for enjoyment of sexual activity.

A similar study conducted at the Duke Center for the Study of Aging revealed that the most accurate predictor of an active sexual life in older age is an active sex life in the earlier years. The Duke researchers found that after seventy-eight years of age, women showed more interest in sex than men did, though, ironically, older women appeared to become less sexually active at a faster rate than men.

There were a variety of reasons why sexual interest often exceeded sexual activity, including illness, a living situation not conducive to sexual activity, decreased desire on the part of a mate, or lack of a partner altogether. In fact, the lack of a sanctioned partner is a barrier to sexual enjoyment in later life for many women. A woman who reaches sixty-five can expect to live for another nineteen years; a man at sixty-five is expected to live only fourteen years. In addition, most women marry older men, thereby increasing the chances and the number of years of widowhood. (According to the survey, married women in the postmenopausal age group were more sexually active than their single counterparts.)

It is perfectly natural for a widowed, divorced, or never-married woman in this age group to feel the same aches of frustration and hunger for love and touching that a younger woman might experience. Research is revealing that human sexuality is lifelong, beginning early in childhood, changing in nature and expression, but continuing throughout life. The stereotype of sexless middle-aged and older women is disappearing as their continuing sexual needs are acknowledged. However, our society still tends to diminish the sexual needs of this population.

None of the physical changes discussed elsewhere in this book have any significant effect on the capacity of a menopausal woman to be an adequate, loving, sexual partner. Menopause is only the end of the menstrual phase of your life; it is not the end of your libido or sexual needs. In one sense, a middle-aged woman is sexually more advantaged than a middle-aged man, in that she remains responsive, whereas a man's ability to attain an erection or achieve orgasm may diminish.

Sexual Responsiveness

Despite the hormonal and anatomical changes that occur with menopause, orgasmic response remains possible. The clitoris does not change, and its function as a sensory organ remains intact. Although a woman may have complaints of vaginal dryness, the ability to achieve orgasm does not diminish. However, the time it takes for lubrication to begin may increase from the thirty seconds following stimulation of the early years to between three and five minutes.

Recent research confirms that middle-aged and older women retain their sexual responsiveness. In one report, which surveyed 800 adults between the ages of sixty and ninety, a large number reported that sex was better than ever. Many women identified orgasms as essential to the sexual experience, and said their orgasms were even more intense than in their youth. These women said they enjoyed nudity with their partners, and revealed that their fantasized "ideal" lover was close to their own age. Both male and female respondents noted that giving pleasure rather than aiming for orgasm relieved them of the pressure to perform and freed them to experience the joy of relating. Most of the women surveyed recognized that they had at least as much passion and sexual desire as their partners.

Sexual Expression

Remember that sexual activity can encompass more than just sexual intercourse: intimacy, love, playing, caring, and touching are all expressions of human sensuality. These needs never change, and do not require the perfect body of youth to be fulfilled. Sexual intercourse may not even be a part of lovemaking eventually. What is important is the intimate relationship between partners.

A survey conducted by *Consumer Reports* found that men and women between the ages of fifty and ninety express their sexuality in a variety of ways. Some rely on oral and manual stimulation of the breasts, genitals, and anus; others use lubricants and vibrators; still others use sexually explicit or pornographic materials and fantasy. Some men and women experiment with various positions for sexual intercourse and with various times of the day. Some employ the technique of inserting the man's partially erect penis into the woman's vagina, both to aid the man's arousal and to gratify the woman. Many of the people surveyed were sexually active, and the levels of enjoyment, variety, and quality of their sexual activity were surprising. Age alone was not enough to eliminate interest and pleasure in sex for most respondents.

Of course, heterosexual intercourse is not the only way to fulfill one's sexual needs. Masturbation is as acceptable a form of sexual expression in the postmenopausal years as it is earlier in life. The stigma attached to this practice has been fading. In fact, self-stimulation can help maintain the sexual responsiveness of the genital organs in addition to relieving tension, increasing sexual desire, and making one feel better in general. However, masturbation is no substitute for sharing with a loving, caring partner.

Homosexuality is also part of the normal range of human sexual behavior, and the stigma associated with lesbianism is also diminishing. Lesbians may even have an advantage over non-lesbians later in life, because the relative number of eligible partners is potentially larger for them than for heterosexual women.

However she chooses to express her sexuality, the middle-aged woman has enormous potential in all roles—professional, wife, mother, lover. The outdated idea of the asexual older woman is now being attributed to unnecessary emotional and physical deprivation. It is now clear that the need for intimate relationships exists throughout life, especially during the middle and later years.

Specific Sexual Problems after Menopause

Though sexuality does not diminish with age, certain physical problems common in the later years can lead to sexual dysfunction. Men can lose their ability to achieve erection and to ejaculate; they can also lose their sexual desire. In women, decreased vaginal lubrication can make sex difficult and possibly painful. These problems, in turn, can also lead to decreased libido; after all, who wants to put herself in a painful situation? Chronic illnesses such as heart conditions, arthritis, and diabetes, which are more prevalent in older age, may also contribute to a couple's sexual problems.

Many older men and women are uneducated about the sexual changes that occur with aging. They persist in believing that vaginal intercourse is the only legitimate form of sex, and that other intimate exchanges such as oral sex, manual stimulation, and masturbation are indecent. In addition, many older couples are reluctant to discuss their sexual needs with each other or with health professionals, leading to frustration and possibly abstinence. Physicians should directly discuss possible sexual problems. If they do not, patients should raise the issue.

Factors contributing to sexual problems in postmenopausal women include physical changes to the vagina, gynecologic surgery, chronic illness, drug treatment, poor physical fitness, or fear. The most common complaints are decreased sexual desire and painful intercourse.

Decreased Sexual Desire

Both medical and psychological factors may contribute to a decrease in sexual desire in some menopausal women. Many women have had unsatisfactory sexual relationships for their entire lives and see menopause as a time when they are no longer expected to be sexually involved. Other women, because of religious or social influences, believe that sexual activity is inappropriate except for the purpose of reproduction. Many women also repress their own sexual desires, responding only to their partner's sexual needs.

Earlier generations of women were taught to be passive participants in sex, never initiating it. Thus, when a woman's spouse was no longer able to perform sexually—or lost his desire to—a woman was expected to accept the situation without considering alternatives. Unfortunately, some couples who can no longer engage in vaginal intercourse discontinue all forms of sexual intimacy, including kissing and holding.

Sexuality is also significantly affected by the aging woman's overall health. Many chronic illnesses, such as heart and lung disease and cancer, can affect sexual function. Cardiopulmonary disease may cause chest pain, trouble with breathing, or the inability to maintain a particular position. Cancer treatments can be debilitating. Anticipation of the problems associated with these illnesses may lead to diminished desire.

In addition, cancer surgery, such as mastectomy or hysterectomy, can affect a woman's concept of her femininity, also leading to decreased desire. Surgical procedures such as breast reconstruction after mastectomy, as well as appropriate counseling and encouragement, can reduce the impact. So can education. The uterus is not essential to sexual enjoyment, though some couples believe it is. (Some experts believe that the cervix, or mouth of the uterus, enhances vaginal sensation during orgasm, and suggest not removing it during hysterectomy to avoid changes in sexual function, but this is controversial.)

Painful Intercourse

Some women report a decrease in vaginal lubrication that may begin early in their forties, even while they are still menstruating. As the ovaries produce less estrogen, vaginal secretions may diminish. The loss of this moisture can result in vaginal discomfort during intercourse, sometimes promoting irritation or infection. Hormone replacement therapy can cause marked relief for vaginal dryness. (If this is the only indication for hormone treatment, some physicians recommend local hormonal gels, which cause fewer side effects than the oral form of treatment. However, because dosages are harder to control with the creams, we prefer to use the oral preparations.) Vaginal lubricants like Astroglide, Replens, or K-Y jelly are also helpful.

If a woman expects pain on intercourse, she may involuntarily contract her vaginal muscles in anticipation of that pain, thereby increasing discomfort and setting up a negative feedback cycle. Her partner may feel reluctant to engage in intercourse for fear of hurting her, which may affect his erectile functioning. Fear of painful intercourse may also lead to abstinence—and it is well-known that continued sexual activity is important for the maintenance of vaginal health. Continued vaginal intercourse serves to stretch the vaginal muscles and skin as well as toughen up the lining.

As physicians, our role is to identify these sexual problems and provide the appropriate counseling and treatment. Patients should communicate openly with both their partner and their physician about any sexual difficulties they are experiencing. Changing sexual routines can alleviate many problems. Intimacy is often more successful and gratifying for older couples in the morning, when they have more energy, than at night. Taking a warm bath can often relieve pain stemming from stiffness of the joints. Engaging in sexual activities other than intercourse can help to alleviate anxiety and enable older people to better enjoy their sexual relations.

6

Cardiovascular Disease
and Menopause

Menopause does not cause heart disease. But the loss of estrogen, which appears to protect women against cardiovascular disease during the premenopausal years, may significantly increase a woman's cardiovascular risk. Women develop heart disease about ten years later than men do. Indeed, it is only recently that experts have recognized that being a postmenopausal woman is as major a heart disease risk factor as being a man. The truth is, cardiovascular disease is the leading cause of death in women, just as it is in men. Unfortunately, because of a sex bias in medical research (researchers have only recently begun studying women on a large-scale basis), information on women and heart disease is sorely lacking. As a result, women's heart symptoms are often missed, and when heart disease is diagnosed in women, it is treated less aggressively than it is in men.

If you are a postmenopausal woman, you must recognize that you are at risk for heart disease. The degree of your risk depends on several factors, which we discuss later in this chapter. One out of three women age sixty-five or older has some form of cardiovascular disease. By making certain lifestyle changes now, you may be able to avoid becoming another statistic.

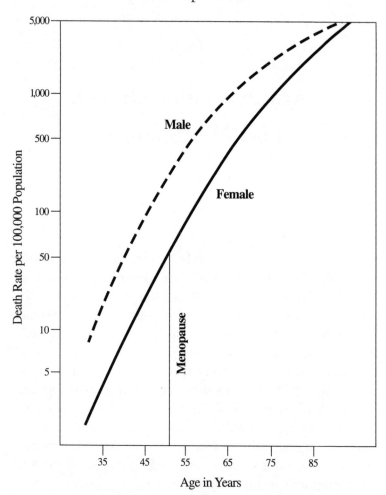

FIGURE 5 *Male and female death rates from coronary heart disease.*
The rates approach each other with advancing age.

What Causes Heart Disease?

The most common and dangerous form of cardiovascular disease is *coronary artery disease,* or closure of the arteries that supply blood to your heart. As people age, the diameter of the

coronary arteries narrows due to the buildup of artery-clogging plaque. This plaque cannot simply be scraped off; it penetrates into the layers of the arterial wall and hardens there, occluding the vessel.

Arteriosclerosis is the general term for hardening of the arteries; the plaque buildup that we are talking about here is caused by the accumulation of cholesterol deposits known as *atherosclerosis*. (Atherosclerosis is a type of arteriosclerosis.) When the artery is blocked, blood cannot reach the heart to deliver the oxygen that is vital to its function. Thus, some of the heart muscle dies and becomes scar tissue, affecting the ability of the heart to contract.

Plaque buildup is not the only means by which coronary arteries can become obstructed. Sometimes the wall of the artery contracts, causing the artery to go into spasm. A sudden spasm can lead to a heart attack. This explains why young women who do not have atherosclerosis can still get heart attacks, though they are rare in women under fifty.

An artery can also become obstructed when a clot forms in a larger vessel in the body and then floats through the artery system, engaging in the smaller coronary artery and occluding it.

Who Is at Risk?

Risk factors can be divided into those that can be modified and those that cannot. Genetic or family history and gender are, of course, part of the hand one is dealt at birth. Nor can one do anything about one's age, which is an important factor for heart disease risk. Risk factors that can be modified, or at least controlled, include diet (cholesterol levels and fat intake, in particular), cigarette smoking, high blood pressure, diabetes, obesity, stress, and a sedentary lifestyle. All of these factors interact to influence your overall risk. A fat, sedentary male who smokes and has a poor cardiac family history, for example, would be at higher risk than a thin, athletic woman who doesn't smoke.

The following is a summary of heart disease risk factors:

Genetic history. If your mother or father had a heart attack at a young age (before age fifty-five), your risk of having one may be as much as five times greater than average, based on this factor alone.

Known heart disease (atherosclerosis). If you have already had one heart attack, you are twice as likely to have another. A woman who has had a heart attack becomes just as likely as a man to have another one, no matter what her age. About one-third of people under fifty who have a heart attack show evidence of a previous problem that went undiagnosed. This underscores the value of routine electrocardiograms on an annual basis over age forty-five. (However, keep in mind that this diagnostic tool is less accurate in women than it is in men; false positives are common in women. A positive finding in a woman will probably need to be confirmed by a more involved stress test.)

High blood pressure. The presence of high blood pressure doubles your risk of a heart attack. A blood pressure reading above 160/95 is considered high. A systolic pressure (the top number) of 120 or lower, and a diastolic pressure (the bottom figure) of no more than 80 is desirable. High blood pressure can be kept in check by medication, diet, and weight control.

Cholesterol and other lipid levels. Your total cholesterol is the first important measurement. Based on studies in men, levels below 200 are desirable; levels above 240 are associated with increased risk of heart attack. Your cholesterol picture is incomplete, however, without measurements of the major lipoproteins that carry cholesterol through the body.

High-density lipoprotein (HDL), which is sometimes referred to as the "good cholesterol," acts as a scavenger of cholesterol, which it carries in the bloodstream. Low-density lipoprotein (LDL) is known as the "bad cholesterol," as it allows cholesterol to settle into plaque on the vessels. There is a direct relationship between elevated levels of LDL and subsequent heart attacks; the higher your HDL level, on the other hand, the lower your heart attack risk. HDL levels of less than 35 may double your risk of heart attack. LDL levels should be less than 130; levels above 160 also increase your heart attack risk. More significant than any of these individual numbers, however, is the ratio of total cholesterol to HDL: a ratio of 4.5 or more indicates increased risk.

Women tend to have an advantage when it comes to cholesterol—at least premenopausally. Because estrogen tends to increase good cholesterol, HDLs run higher in women: about 50, compared to about 40 in men. Women lose this advantage after menopause, however, unless they take estrogen (we return to this in chapter 8).

Smoking. Smoking increases cardiovascular risk at any age. Few young women have heart attacks, but those who do are much more likely to be smokers. Smoking lowers your levels of good cholesterol, or HDL.

Diabetes. Diabetes doubles your risk of heart disease. Several studies suggest, however, that good diabetic control can reduce the significance of this risk factor.

Overweight. Being overweight significantly increases one's risk of heart disease. But not all fat is created equal: women who tend to accumulate fat around the abdomen are at higher risk than those who collect fat in the hips and buttocks. Whatever your body shape, you are at lowest risk if you are below your ideal weight (see table 6 on page 128).

Sedentary lifestyle. Women who do not exercise are more likely to suffer heart attacks. Exercise helps to reduce weight, raises your HDL, lowers your LDL, and helps control your general metabolism. Studies have shown that simply exercising three times a week, for a half hour, will get your heart rate up to a level that increases its efficiency (see chapter 11 on exercise).

Stress. We all remember the studies showing that the Type A personality—an obsessive overachiever who experiences a great deal of stress—is at increased risk. Researchers have also demonstrated a relationship between stressful life events (for example, family death, divorce, and job change) and coronary disease and death. One study also suggested that postmenopausal women had more dramatic physiologic responses to stress than either premenopausal women or men.

Age. The older you get, the more you are at risk for heart disease. One in nine women ages forty-five to sixty-four has some form of cardiovascular disease; that ratio jumps to one in three for women sixty-five and over. The National Cholesterol Education Program recently added postmenopausal status to its guidelines for increased heart disease risk.

Estrogen and Heart Disease

We do not know for sure how estrogen helps to protect premenopausal women from heart disease, though there are several theories. We know that estrogens increase HDL levels, but we believe that this is only part of the story. Estrogen may also have a beneficial effect on the blood vessels that lead to the heart, increasing blood flow and maintaining the ability of the arterial walls to relax and expand (this is known as *vasodilation*).

Considering that estrogen seems to protect premenopausal women from heart disease, it stands to reason that estrogen given to postmenopausal women might do the same. There has never been a good clinical trial on the effect of hormone replacement therapy on cardiovascular disease, but there are several epidemiologic studies that have noted benefits. (An epidemiologic study surveys a large population of subjects, some of whom may be using hormones, for example, and retrospectively looks for associations between hormone use and disease; a clinical trial would follow subjects prospectively, watching to see whether women taking hormones eventually develop disease. The latter type of study holds more scientific weight.)

The Nurses Health Study at Harvard University, administered in the past decade, was one of the largest studies to report a positive finding: researchers showed that current estrogen users had a 70 percent reduced risk of coronary heart disease. In the past five years, there have been several other studies suggesting a 50 to 80 percent reduced risk of heart disease and stroke among women who use estrogen. These studies all showed that current use (as opposed to past use) offers the greatest protection against cardiovascular disease. In other words, estrogen must be used long-term to provide the greatest cardiovascular benefits.

There are also a number of studies showing that estrogen may protect women who have had previous cardiovascular disease from recurrence. The investigators who conducted these studies have suggested using estrogen as a preventive agent once a woman has already had a heart attack.

The evidence is tempting, but the problem is that we have

added progesterone to the equation of estrogen replacement therapy in order to prevent endometrial cancer. Many of the studies demonstrating the protective effect of hormone replacement against heart disease were conducted before we routinely used progesterone. We know that progesterone can lower HDL levels—not a good idea—and we therefore suspect that progesterone may counteract the beneficial cardiovascular effects of estrogen.

Some experts say that if estrogen works in ways other than raising HDL, its positive cardiovascular effects might outweigh the negative effects of progesterone on blood lipids. In fact, the National Institutes of Health has two large studies under way that will compare the effects of estrogen alone and estrogen with progesterone on heart disease risk, among other things. For now, however, progesterone is the wild card, an unknown.

How does this leave us? Women should be aware of the potential benefits and risks of taking both unopposed estrogen (without progesterone) and combined hormone therapy. (See chapter 8 on hormones.) As it stands today, postmenopausal women should not be taking hormones as the sole method of preventing heart disease until the possible adverse effects of estrogen or progesterone are determined. Women should take other steps to prevent heart disease, with or without hormone therapy.

Reducing Heart Disease Risk

By making some simple life-style changes, you can significantly reduce your risk of heart disease. Kicking the cigarette habit is a big step in the right direction. Ex-smokers lose their high-risk status within two to three years of quitting. When a person stops smoking, her HDL levels usually rise, improving the cholesterol picture as well.

Eating a healthful, low-fat diet and exercising regularly take care of several risk factors at once. Not only does exercise directly condition the cardiovascular system, but it also raises HDLs and helps lose or maintain weight. Cutting down on dietary fat will also contribute to weight loss, since there are twice as many calories in a gram of fat as in a gram of carbohydrate or protein. It is also possible to improve your cholesterol profile through dietary changes.

Most experts recommend keeping fat intake below 30 percent of total calories consumed. Fat can be replaced in the diet with complex carbohydrates such as whole grains. One approach is to cut down on intake of meat and high-fat dairy products, since saturated fat, the kind found in animal products, is the most significant dietary component affecting blood cholesterol. In fact, people in Japan, who eat much less saturated fat than we do in the United States, tend to have a significantly lower incidence of heart disease. Researchers have found that when Japanese people move to the United States and assume the high-fat American diet, their cholesterol levels and heart attack incidence increase to American proportions.

If you have a history of heart disease in your family, discuss the option of aspirin therapy with your physician. This may be a better alternative than hormone replacement therapy.

We discuss diet and exercising strategies in more detail in chapters 11 and 12.

7

Your Bones and Menopause

Osteoporosis is a condition in which the bones get progressively thinner, and therefore more fragile, with age. Most of us reach our peak bone density by the time we are thirty; a gradual loss of bone mass begins shortly thereafter. Menopause (and the accompanying decline in estrogen production) accelerates this process, sometimes leading to significantly weakened, brittle bones that are extremely susceptible to fractures.

Both the degree and rate of bone loss around menopause vary markedly from person to person. The process of bone loss does not produce symptoms and is of little consequence until many years later, when suddenly there may be a fracture. Such fractures—most commonly of the hip, wrist, or spine—are fairly prevalent among postmenopausal women.

It is clear that menopause is one factor in producing osteoporosis. In fact, about 25 percent of women will have some X-ray evidence of the bone disease by age sixty-five. Thus, by the year 2000, we can expect at least five million women in the United States to have osteoporosis. This doesn't mean, however, that five million women will suffer from hip fractures.

About 25 to 50 percent of women reach a critically low level of bone mass by their early sixties, below which the theoretical risk of fracture is increased. The frequency of fractures due to osteoporosis rises with age in both women and men; however, this increase is more pronounced—and occurs earlier—in women. A woman's risk of hip fracture doubles each decade after age fifty. About 1.3 percent of women over the age of sixty-five will suffer from hip fractures each year, compared to .3 percent of men in the same age group. In fact, 85 percent of all hip fractures occur in women.

Over the past few years, the media have turned osteoporosis into a household word. Public awareness of this health problem is good, but it has also created much unwarranted anxiety in the elderly female population. The image of a bent-over old woman with a dowager's hump has been used in advertisements and the media as a symbol of osteoporosis. Despite the prevalence of the condition, the end stage of the disease is quite rare. Only occasionally will we see a severely osteoporotic woman—less than 10 percent of women over seventy have vertebral fractures that could eventually lead to the classic dowager's hump.

Drug companies, vitamin supplement manufacturers, and the milk industry, among others, also play up the number of deaths that occur from hip fractures in the elderly. About 10 percent of those suffering from hip fractures die from complications of the surgery or prolonged recovery. This makes hip fractures one of the twelve most common causes of death in the United States. But despite the grim statistics, osteoporosis does not loom so large in the lives of all women.

One study of bone density in postmenopausal women showed that only 7 to 8 percent were at high risk for fractures; 20 percent were at intermediate risk; and 70 percent—the majority—were at low risk. In addition, most of those who die from hip fractures are over eighty years old and have some other debilitating disease that exacerbates the problem. In fact, even though osteoporosis is quite common, most women will not end up crippled by the disease. Most women will never even know they have it.

There is no doubt that hip fractures in the elderly pose a serious problem. Some people are disabled from such fractures, and others die from complications. But osteoporosis is not the only cause of hip fractures, and the idea of the entire female population of the world taking estrogen to prevent osteoporosis simply is not warranted at this time.

Who Is at Risk?

We all lose bone mass as we get older. The degree of age-related osteoporosis, however, depends on three basic factors:

Sex. Women have an acceleration of bone loss immediately following menopause, especially if they have premature or surgical menopause. By the time their rate of bone loss slows to the same rate as men's (around age sixty-five), women's bone density is considerably less than men's.

Genetics. White women and Asian women are more prone to osteoporosis than African-American women; a thin or petite body type also predisposes one to the bone disease. Family history of osteoporosis puts one at increased risk as well.

Lifestyle. Smoking, excessive alcohol intake, excessive caffeine, lack of exercise, certain medications (steroids, anti-inflammatory drugs, some epilepsy drugs, excess thyroid hormone), and poor nutrition—particularly, inadequate calcium intake—all promote osteoporosis.

Bone Metabolism

Calcium is required for the production and formation of bone, so adequate calcium in the diet is crucial to maintaining bone strength. Though one generally stops adding to one's bone mass by age thirty, dietary calcium remains important, because when the body does not get enough calcium, it leaches the mineral from bones, accelerating the natural decline in bone density. (Bone undergoes a process of continual turnover throughout life: small quantities of bone are resorbed by the body so that calcium can be released for use by other body tissues, and then osteoblasts, or bone-building cells, rebuild the bone. When the body does not get enough calcium, bone is resorbed faster than it can be repaired.)

Exercise is another important factor in developing and maintaining strong bones: stressing the bones encourages growth, making bones thicker, whereas inactivity spurs bone loss. Healthful eating combined with regular, weight-bearing exercise in the years prior to menopause will help ensure that you enter this phase of life with the greatest possible bone density.

As we mentioned earlier, a gradual decline in bone mass occurs between the fourth and sixth decades of life. The most rapid bone loss occurs in the first five years after menopause, presumably because of the sudden drop in estrogen production. The role that estrogen plays in bone metabolism is not precisely known, though it appears to be involved in creating a support system for calcium deposition.

There is no evidence that estrogen influences the bone directly—no receptors for estrogen have ever been found in bone. It is assumed that estrogens work indirectly by their effect on three other body substances: calcitonin, parathyroid hormone, and vitamin D. Most experts feel that estrogen stimulates the production of calcitonin, which prevents bone resorption and enhances bone formation. Studies have shown that estrogen replacement can prevent the acceleration of bone loss that occurs at menopause, as well as reduce the incidence of osteoporotic fractures. However, bone loss will accelerate again once estrogen is stopped. Therefore, taking estrogen for the first ten years following menopause will not protect against fractures twenty or thirty years later.

Bone Fractures

The most common types of fractures occur in the wrist, vertebrae (or spine), and hip.

Wrist fractures usually occur when a woman extends her arm to break a fall. They generally heal easily and do not lead to subsequent disability. Wrist fractures are not always associated with osteoporosis.

Vertebral fractures occur spontaneously, as the weakened vertebrae simply collapse under the weight of the body. Lifting heavy objects, making sudden movements, or exercising intensely can contribute to vertebral fractures. As the vertebrae collapse, the spine compresses downward and shortens in length, causing the characteristic loss of height that often comes with aging. In the worst case scenario, the whole spine curves, causing the dowager's hump.

Women are generally unaware that they have a fracture of the spine; it is usually discovered incidentally when X rays are taken for some other reason. Occasionally, there is sharp pain at the site of the fracture, but the pain passes as the acute fracture heals, usually within a week or two. Osteoporosis commonly leads to vertebral fracture. Contributing factors, however, include an increased rate of falling among the elderly due to a lack of physical fitness and perhaps impaired cognitive functions.

Hip fractures are potentially the most serious, because they can take a long time to heal. An operation is sometimes necessary to pin the bone so that the patient will not have to be immobilized during the long healing process. In rare cases, pneumonia or blood clots result from prolonged bed rest and can lead to death. Those who die from hip fractures are usually quite elderly, and may have preexisting illnesses. Still, doctors now advise moving soon after treatment of a hip fracture to avoid the complications associated with extended bed rest.

A hip fracture can be devastating, causing considerable loss of mobility and independence. Most who suffer them recover, however, except for the very elderly and debilitated. Osteoporosis is not the sole cause of hip fractures. Bone aging and the propensity to fall with older age are also factors.

Measuring Bone Density

Since degree of bone density is related to the risk of fractures, we can predict fracture risk by measuring bone density. Early methods used X rays to measure bone density in the wrist or heel. However, it is unclear whether measuring bone density in one part of the body—particularly in the appendages, where bone loss is more subtle—can accurately predict the likelihood of fractures in other bones in the body.

Currently, the most accurate way of measuring bone density is a technique called *dexa bone densitometry*. This method, which also uses X rays, can measure bone mass in the spine or hip, both of which are more significant in terms of osteoporosis, as well as in any other site in the body. With this method there is also very little exposure to radiation. Computerized axial tomography (CAT) scans can also measure bone in the spine, but are quite expensive compared to dexa bone densitometry.

Should all women be screened after menopause for their risk for osteoporosis? Some experts suggest screening only high-risk women, such as those with a family history of osteoporosis, or thin white or Asian women. However, this would miss many women who would be at risk. Other experts suggest screening all women after menopause for bone density. Whether this would be cost-effective or not is unknown, but the advantage would be that only those at moderate to high risk would have to be treated with estrogen replacement therapy or other medications. We believe that bone density studies are particularly useful in monitoring bone loss in postmenopausal women who are not on hormone replacement therapy. If these women start showing signs of osteoporosis, hormones can be reconsidered.

Prevention of Osteoporosis

If you are premenopausal, you can keep bones strong and stave off osteoporosis by consuming adequate amounts of calcium, exercising regularly, quitting smoking, and minimizing alcohol intake. These measures become even more important once you hit menopause and bone loss accelerates.

Calcium and Other Dietary Factors

Some of the most convincing evidence of the significance of calcium intake in preventing osteoporosis came from a study carried out in Yugoslavia. Researchers compared the frequency of hip fractures among residents of two villages whose dietary intake of calcium differed significantly. In one village, lifelong calcium intake averaged 1,000 milligrams per day; in the other, residents typically consumed 450 milligrams per day. The rate of hip fractures was markedly lower among the villagers who consumed

TABLE 2
Foods Containing Calcium

FOOD	AMOUNT	CALCIUM (MG)	FAT (G)
Milk and Dairy Products			
American cheese	1 oz.	195	8.4
Cheddar cheese	1 oz.	211	9.1
Swiss cheese	1 oz.	219	7.1
Ice cream, hard	1 cup	176	14.1
Low-fat milk	1 cup	298	4.7
Skim milk	1 cup	303	0.4
Low-fat plain yogurt	1 cup	415	3.4
Nuts			
Almonds, roasted and salted	1 oz.	66	16.2
Sesame seeds, dried, hulled	3 ½ oz.	100	53.4
Seafood			
Scallops, steamed	3 ½ oz.	115	1.4
Shrimp, raw	3 ½ oz.	63	0.8
Green Leafy Vegetables			
Broccoli, cooked	⅔ cup	88	0.3
Kale, cooked, without stems	¾ cup	187	0.7
Spinach, cooked	½ cup	83	0.3
Turnip greens, cooked	⅔ cup	184	0.2
Other Foods			
Chili con carne with beans	5 oz.	61	9.9
Cream of celery soup made with milk	3 oz.	135	33.0
Figs, dried	5 medium	126	1.3
Slice from 12-inch cheese pizza	4" slice	144	4.4
Pudding, chocolate, cornstarch	½ cup	147	6.6
Raisins, dried, seedless	⅝ cup	62	0.2

more calcium. By comparing two Yugoslavian villages, other factors that influence osteoporosis, such as genetics, were presumably controlled.

The recommended daily allowance (RDA) of calcium for premenopausal (nonpregnant) women is 800 milligrams. It is now generally felt that postmenopausal women require additional calcium—about 1,500 milligrams per day. Unfortunately, the average intake of calcium among women in the United States is only 400 to 600 milligrams per day. Therefore, we can assume that most women are deficient in calcium. We cannot overstress the importance of calcium in your diet. (See table 2 for sources of calcium in food.)

Because few women consume adequate calcium, some experts recommend calcium supplements. Various studies have shown that calcium supplementation can prevent deterioration in bones. Few studies, however, take into account that factors other than calcium can affect bone loss. Excessive protein or phosphate intake (phosphates are found in certain heartburn medications such as Amphojel) can accelerate bone loss despite calcium intake. Alcohol and caffeine also promote bone loss.

Though the mineral is vital to bones, calcium alone will not prevent osteoporosis. Bone will not form unless the stimulus of mechanical stress, namely exercise, is present.

Exercise

A simple exercise program of short duration can help maintain bone mineral content (see figure 6). Weight-bearing exercise (such as walking, running, aerobic dancing, or weight training) is most effective in reducing age-related bone loss. Studies have shown that by simply walking or running for one hour, twice a week, you can significantly *increase* the bone mass of your spine. Keep in mind, however, that physical activity is only helpful when there is sufficient calcium intake. We discuss exercise in greater detail in chapter 11.

Hormonal Factors

Repeated pregnancies, breast-feeding, and the use of birth control pills all seem to help prevent osteoporosis, perhaps by maintaining exposure to estrogens over a long period of time. Calcitonin is also stimulated by pregnancy; as we mentioned earlier, this hormone reduces bone absorption and enhances the function of osteoblasts, the cells that produce bone formation.

Increase or Decrease in Bone Mineral Content

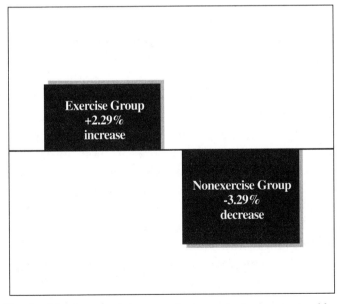

FIGURE 6 *Light to moderate exercise improves bone mass in older women. A study in which older women (mean age 81) did various simple exercises showed increased bone mineral content, while a matched nonexercise group lost bone mineral.*

Estrogen replacement therapy can prevent the rapid bone loss associated with the sudden decline of estrogen. But the causes of osteoporosis are multiple, and bone loss stemming from other factors will continue despite estrogen treatment.

Preventing Falls and Fractures

At any age, injuries from a fall can limit one's ability to lead an active, independent life. The older one is, however, the more likely it is that a fall will cause significant disability. Each year, thousands of elderly people are disabled, sometimes permanently, by falls that result in broken bones. Many of these injuries can be prevented by making simple changes in the home.

As one ages, changes in vision, hearing, muscle strength, coordination, and reflexes may make one more likely to fall. In addition, the older one is, the more likely one is to suffer from disorders that affect balance, such as diabetes, heart conditions, thyroid disease, and nervous system disorders. Older people also take more drugs that can cause dizziness or light-headedness.

Prevention of falls is especially important for people who have osteoporosis, because their bones are more brittle and tend to break easily. For the person with severe osteoporosis, even a minor fall may cause one or more bones to break.

Falls and accidents seldom "just happen." Many can be prevented. There are simple steps one can take to reduce the likelihood of falling and to make the home a safer place. The following are some guidelines for preventing falls and fractures:

- Have your vision and hearing tested regularly and then properly corrected. Even the simple task of removing earwax can improve your balance.
- Talk to your doctor or pharmacist about the side effects of

any drugs you are taking, and ask how they may affect your coordination or balance. Ask for suggestions on how to reduce the possibility of falling.

- Limit your intake of alcohol. Even a little alcohol can further disturb already impaired balance and reflexes.
- Do not get up too quickly after eating, lying down, or resting. Low blood pressure may cause dizziness at these times.
- Make sure that the nighttime temperature in your home is not lower than 65° F. Prolonged exposure to cold temperatures may cause your body temperature to drop, leading to dizziness and falling. Older people cannot tolerate cold as well as younger people.
- If you sometimes feel dizzy, use a cane, walking stick, or walker to help maintain balance. Use special caution in walking outdoors on wet and icy pavement.
- Wear supportive, rubber-soled, low-heeled shoes. Avoid wearing only socks, smooth-soled shoes, or slippers on stairs or waxed floors.
- Maintain a regular exercise program. Regular physical activity improves strength and muscle tone, which will help in moving about more easily by keeping joints, tendons, and ligaments more flexible. Many older people enjoy walking, swimming, and other forms of exercise. Mild weight-bearing activities may even reduce the loss of bone from osteoporosis. It is important, however, to consult your doctor or physical therapist to plan a suitable exercise program.

Beyond these everyday activities, there are also a number of things you can do around your home to prevent falls. Many falls are caused by hazardous conditions in the home.

Safety Checklist for Your Home

Stairways, hallways, and pathways should have:

- Good lighting and no clutter
- Firmly attached carpeting, rough texture, or nonskid strips to secure footing
- Tightly fastened handrails running the entire length and along both sides of all stairs, with light switches at the top and bottom

Bathrooms should have:

- Grab bars conveniently located in and out of tubs and showers and near toilets
- Nonskid mats or strips, or carpeting on all surfaces that may get wet
- Night-lights

Bedrooms should have:

- Night-lights or light switches within reach of the bed(s)
- Easily reached telephones, convenient to the bed(s)

Living areas should have:

- Electrical cords and telephone wires routed away from walking paths
- Rugs well secured to the floor
- Furniture (especially low coffee tables) and other objects arranged so they are not in the way
- Couches and chairs at proper height to get into and out of easily

Treatment of Osteoporosis
Estrogen

It is well established that taking estrogen diminishes post-menopausal osteoporosis, but a woman must take hormones for many years, perhaps to age eighty, to reap this benefit. Studies have shown that postmenopausal women treated with estrogen suffer from fewer bone fractures, but lose this protection if they discontinue the treatment. The dose of estrogen required to achieve this beneficial effect is minor. As little as .3 milligrams of oral estrogen per day will reduce calcium loss in some women; .625 milligrams is the daily dose required to prevent bone loss in all women. The lower dose may be sufficient when supplemented with 1,500 milligrams of calcium daily. In addition, even lower doses of estrogen may be adequate if estrogen therapy is combined with progesterone (which has also been shown to prevent bone loss) and exercise.

If estrogen replacement therapy prevents osteoporosis, should all women take it? The problem is that estrogen replacement therapy has to be pursued for many years in order to prevent osteoporosis. A study in *The New England Journal of Medicine* of October 18, 1993, suggests that estrogen may have to be taken *forever* to prevent fractures. Once a woman stops taking hormones, especially if she is under sixty-five, bone loss will be rapid so that any benefits from hormones may be lost. (Only by the time a woman reaches sixty-five—about fifteen years after menopause—does her bone loss slow to the same rate as that in a man.) After ten years of estrogen replacement therapy, the risks of breast cancer increase.

Another option might be for a woman to start estrogen replacement many years after menopause and continue it for life. Studies show that estrogen can increase bone density by 5 to 10 percent in older women. This improvement in bone density could reduce the risk of fractures by about one-third.

Considering that taking estrogen for just a decade after menopause is unlikely to prevent osteoporosis, we see three possible treatment options.

1. Take estrogen for life.
2. Take estrogen only if there is evidence of osteoporosis or a family tendency for it.
3. Take estrogen starting at age seventy or if a fracture occurs.

Because good habits, good nutrition, calcium supplementation, and exercise also prevent osteoporosis—and these lifestyle measures do not entail risk—we favor the second option.

Other Methods of Treatment

Women who are at risk for—or who already have—osteoporosis have several treatment options that can be used instead of, or in combination with, estrogen replacement therapy. They include progesterone, calcitonin, parathyroid hormone, fluoride, biphosphonates, vitamin D, and possibly tamoxifen. (These medications are discussed in chapter 10, on alternative treatments.)

A number of studies have shown that bone mass will actually increase when progesterone is used with estrogen, though calcium was also used in these studies. Other studies have found that progesterone alone may prevent bone density from decreasing.

Another alternative is to take hormones when X rays indicate early osteoporosis or after osteoporotic fractures occur. This approach targets a high-risk group that is likely to comply with treatment. But it appears that, for osteoporosis *prevention*, starting hormone therapy at age sixty-five would be best.

Recommendations

At this point our recommendations can be summarized as follows:

1. Postmenopausal women who are at high risk for osteoporosis should take estrogen replacement therapy, perhaps for life, if there are no contraindications.
2. Other women can have periodic bone density studies to pick up early osteoporosis, and then begin treatment, if necessary.
3. Women can begin hormone treatment after osteoporotic fractures occur.
4. All postmenopausal women should participate in a prevention program consisting of regular exercise, a balanced diet, and adequate dietary calcium intake or supplementation.

8

Hormonal Treatment of Menopause

Resolving the controversy surrounding hormone replacement therapy is not an easy task. Evidence supporting the safety and effectiveness of hormone use is poor and conflicting. While important ongoing studies may eventually provide some answers, they offer little solace to the woman who is trying to make an informed decision about hormone replacement therapy today.

The existing data raise troubling questions: If a woman takes hormones to prevent osteoporosis, is she putting herself at increased risk for breast cancer? If she opts for combined hormone therapy to protect herself against endometrial cancer, is she negating the medication's heart benefits? If she chooses hormone replacement therapy to alleviate temporary symptoms like hot flashes, is she setting herself up for long-term risks?

Despite the fact that there are still more questions than answers, hormones are already in widespread use. Granted, claims for hormone replacement therapy have not materialized out of thin air—a number of studies have suggested a range of benefits for hormone use. But research from the past is not always applicable to current treatment. Today, doctors prescribe lower dosages of hormones than they did initially, and in different combinations. Because progesterone was only recently added to the equation when it became clear that unopposed estrogen was causing cancer of the uterus, there has not been sufficient time to study the long-term effects of combined therapy.

Ironically, there is a tendency for proponents of hormone replacement therapy to use the benefits of the older studies to promote hormone use, yet they dismiss complications on the grounds that the hormonal preparations used in previous studies are not used today. They cannot have it both ways. When reeling off the benefits of hormone treatment, proponents also tend to use the term estrogen replacement therapy indiscriminately to refer to both estrogen alone and the more commonly used combined estrogen-progesterone therapy. But the distinction is important. Unopposed estrogen, for example, may lower cholesterol and raise high-density lipoprotein (HDL), whereas combined therapy may not.

Yet another flaw in the research used to back up hormone replacement therapy claims is that different forms of estrogen and progesterone are used in different countries around the world, and some studies lump the various types of hormone replacement therapy together in discussing their results. It is not clear, for example, that oral estrogen, which probably acts on lipids as it passes through the liver, affects the body in the same way as the transdermal estrogen (the patch), which is absorbed through the skin directly into the bloodstream, bypassing the liver.

The History of Estrogen

The concept of hormone therapy dates back to at least Egyptian times, when ovarian extracts were first used to replace estrogen. A renewal of this form of treatment occurred in Berlin in 1896, when doctors, inspired by the successful treatment of thyroid deficiency with thyroid extract, prescribed crude ovarian preparations for a variety of ailments. Use of these preparations was widespread, though the indications were quite varied. Responses to the medication were variable as well, because many of the extracts exhibited extremely low estrogenic activity. It was not until 1900, when researchers transplanted ovaries into male rabbits, that the ovary was shown to be a hormone-producing organ.

In 1929, researchers isolated the hormone *estrone* from the urine of a pregnant woman, and standardized estrogen preparations became available. The first American study to demonstrate the successful use of estrogen to treat menopausal symptoms was published in 1935. Several different estrogen preparations came onto the market in the years that followed, though it was not until the physician Robert Wilson's *Feminine Forever* popularized the idea of estrogen replacement in the early 1960s that hormones became as widely prescribed as they are today.

Currently, the most frequently used estrogen preparation is Premarin, made by Ayerst Laboratories, though several other pharmaceutical companies have similar products on the market. Extracted from the urine of pregnant mares, these "conjugated equine estrogens" are readily absorbed orally. Estrogens are also administered intravaginally (using vaginal creams) and transdermally (via skin patches).

Progesterone

Following the discovery in the late 1970s that unopposed estrogen significantly increases (by eight times) the risk of endometrial cancer, manufacturers began adding progesterone to the estrogen regimen. The combined therapy eliminated the problem of uterine cancer. We now routinely add progesterone to hormone replacement therapy, unless a woman has undergone a hysterectomy. In this case, progesterone may not be used because of a presumed adverse effect on lipids, which could conceivably negate a major proposed benefit of estrogen replacement, namely, the prevention of cardiovascular disease. In addition, progesterone seems to produce significant side effects resembling premenstrual syndrome (PMS) in some women. However, with adjustments in dosage, type of progesterone, or frequency of administration, most women can tolerate progesterone without adverse reaction.

Hormone Replacement Regimens

There are basically three regimens that most physicians use:

1. Estrogen alone (or unopposed estrogen).
2. Sequential treatment, where a period of estrogen use is followed by a shorter period of combined estrogen-progesterone therapy (this method mimics the menstrual cycle).
3. Continuous combined therapy, with both estrogen and progesterone given simultaneously.

Many combinations of hormone therapies are being used. Most physicians have their own particular favorite, which unfortunately complicates research on the safety of the various regimens. A common approach is to minimize risk but preserve effectiveness by utilizing the lowest dose necessary to obtain the desired result. This means the quantity of hormone given should be sufficient to relieve any symptoms, as well as adequate from a preventive-medicine point of view. The minimum dose of Premarin should be .625 milligrams for twenty-one to twenty-

five days per cycle. Smaller amounts of estrogen can often relieve the vaginal and vasomotor symptoms, but will not prevent
osteoporotic bone loss in all women.

Unopposed Estrogen

Unopposed estrogen is usually reserved for those women who
have had a hysterectomy, due to the increased risk of endometrial
cancer. However, some doctors are beginning to argue in favor
of unopposed estrogen for all women, because it is so effective
in preventing cardiovascular disease. They mention that a simple endometrial biopsy can be performed annually to look for
early evidence of endometrial cancer. However, this technique
is sometimes painful, not always accurate, and often expensive.
Another argument made by these doctors is that the cancer that
women get from unopposed estrogen treatment is not a "bad
cancer," as it is highly curable. Well, we think that any cancer is
a bad cancer, and we currently recommend that only women who
have had a hysterectomy or who absolutely cannot tolerate progesterone be given unopposed estrogen. (The latter will require
the annual endometrial sampling.)

Sequential Treatment

With sequential therapy, estrogen is usually taken for two weeks,
and progesterone is added on the fifteenth day of the cycle for
ten days. Upon withdrawal of estrogen and progesterone on the
twenty-fifth day of the cycle, menstrual-like bleeding occurs.
This withdrawal bleeding prevents the buildup of the uterine
lining, which could eventually lead to cancer. The hormone
doses used vary among physicians, but the classic regimen calls
for a daily .625 milligram dose of Premarin from day one to day
twenty-five, with a daily 10 milligram dose of Provera added on

day fifteen for ten days. Beginning the medication on the first day of the month makes it easier to keep track of which pills to take each day.

Continuous Combined Therapy

The problem with sequential therapy is that it eliminates what many women consider the highlight of menopause: the end of the menstrual period. Because many women do not want to continue to have periods, a new method of drug treatment has been devised to avoid withdrawal bleeding while still protecting the endometrium. Currently, continuous combined therapy is the most widely used regimen.

Initially, however, women on continuous therapy do get irregular bleeding. The bleeding lasts until the lining of the uterus becomes very thin, a process that takes approximately six months. This side effect is frustrating to patients (who cannot predict when the bleeding will occur) and a source of concern for physicians, since it can mask signs of endometrial cancer (which is usually detected because of abnormal bleeding). The advantage of this method is that less progesterone can be used. A common daily regimen is .625 milligrams of Premarin and 2.5 milligrams of Provera. The lower dose is thought to diminish some of the PMS-like symptoms associated with the quantities of progesterone used on the sequential schedule. The continuous method is relatively new, so it has not yet been widely studied.

Different Types of Estrogens

Estrogen for patient use comes in three forms: oral, transdermal, and vaginal.

Oral Estrogens

Premarin, the most widely used estrogen preparation in the United States, comes in doses of .3, .625, .9, and 1.25 milligrams taken orally. Stored in—and slowly released by—the fatty tissue, this type of estrogen is potent and long-acting. The effects of Premarin are usually seen within one month of beginning treatment. Other oral estrogens include Ogen and Estrace; as far as we can determine at this time, their effects are similar to those of Premarin.

Transdermal Estrogens

Estraderm, which was introduced to the market in 1988, is a skin patch that contains estradiol (a synthetic estrogen) in its purest form. This small adhesive patch is applied to the skin like a Band-Aid (it is usually worn on the lower abdomen) and releases estrogen over a period of three days, after which another patch is applied. Some women develop irritation at the site of the patch, in which case they can move it to another area. Sometimes itching is severe enough to require the use of another method.

Because transdermal estrogen is absorbed through the skin and directly into the bloodstream, bypassing the intestinal tract and liver, it may eliminate certain side effects. (For example, oral estrogen thickens bile in the liver before it reaches the gallbladder, sometimes leading to gall stones.) Women with gallbladder disease might want to consider this method. On the other hand, because it bypasses the liver, it may not have the same beneficial effect on the lipids. Women who have not had a hysterectomy must take oral progesterone, since it is not yet available in a transdermal patch.

An estrogen gel, which is spread over a wide area of the abdomen and thighs every other day, is available in France. But levels of absorption vary from woman to woman, and are difficult to measure. For this reason, the method has not become popular in the United States.

Vaginal Estrogens

Dienestrol cream and Premarin cream are two vaginal creams prescribed for estrogen use. They immediately produce a high concentration of estrogen in the vagina and are therefore particularly helpful in treating atrophic changes. The creams are initially applied three to four times per week, but can be used less frequently once vaginal symptoms improve. The creams take up to two months to work. In addition to acting on local tissues, the creams are also absorbed through the vaginal walls into the bloodstream. It is difficult to tell how much of the estrogen actually enters the bloodstream, so its effect on the body is not well-known. We prefer to treat with the oral or patch methods, because we can prescribe a known dose and still preserve the effect on the vagina.

How Long Should Treatment Be Used?

Optimum length of treatment, too, is an unknown. Some physicians treat initially to diminish the symptoms of menopause, and then slowly decrease the dosage so that the patient will pass slowly through this transition phase with a minimum of symptoms. With this approach, medication can be stopped within two or three years.

Other physicians are of the school that hormone replacement should be used for decades, if not for life, to prevent osteoporosis and cardiovascular disease. This doctrine has nothing to do with symptomatic menopause. It has to do with the view of menopause as a deficiency disease. And though prospective studies on the use of hormone replacement to prevent heart disease and osteoporosis have not yet been completed, the belief that hormones should be taken indefinitely for just this purpose is very prevalent in our society.

What physicians consider the "safe" period for hormone replacement use has been stretched from five or six years to fifteen years or more, especially since recent epidemiological studies have suggested that prevention of osteoporosis requires at least fifteen years of use. We advise caution. Our point of view stresses (1) the unknown effects of long-term estrogen replacement on the breasts, (2) the alternatives to hormone therapy for prevention of osteoporosis, and (3) the diminished cardiovascular effects of estrogen when progesterone is added.

Despite the fact that many gynecologists are encouraging long-term use of hormones, no one can claim yet that long-term hormone therapy is 100 percent safe. In fact, the little available long-term data point to an increasing cancer risk with duration of use. It is our opinion that, at this point in time, hormone replacement is not indicated for postmenopausal women across the board.

The Risks of Hormone Replacement

What are the safety concerns? Because the current hormone replacement regimens have not been around for that long, we still do not have a clear picture regarding long-term risks of hormone use. Until more research is done, all we can do is weigh the possible benefits of hormone replacement therapy against what little is known about potential adverse effects.

Endometrial Cancer

Many studies have shown that unopposed estrogen can cause excess stimulation of the uterine lining, leading to hyperplasia (overproduction of cells) and eventually endometrial cancer. The use of progesterone, however, markedly decreases this risk. In fact, the use of the combined treatment lowers the risk of endometrial cancer below that of a postmenopausal woman who is not taking hormones.

Breast Cancer

Breast cancer is the big unknown with regard to hormone replacement therapy. Several studies have suggested that long-term use of hormones increases a woman's risk of breast cancer, though other studies have yielded conflicting results. (This research is discussed in more detail in chapter 13 on breast cancer.) Breast cancer is the most common cancer in women, affecting about one in eight women in the United States. It is most prevalent among midlife and older women. Because of the large numbers of women in this age group taking hormone replacement therapy, even a slight increase in breast cancer due to hormone use would be quite significant. We do not recommend hormone replacement therapy for women who have a family history of breast cancer. The current thinking is that taking estrogen for fifteen years or more increases breast cancer risk by 30 percent.

Gallbladder Disease

Bile, which helps in the digestion of food, is produced by the liver and stored in the gallbladder. Unless estrogen is given transdermally, the hormone passes through the liver before entering the bloodstream, where it can thicken and concentrate the bile, increasing the risk of gallstones. These gallstones can cause infection and irritation in the gallbladder. They can also obstruct the flow of bile into the intestinal tract. Studies have shown that women using estrogen are two and a half times more likely to get gallbladder disease than women who do not take hormones.

Blood Clots

Women using estrogen for birth control (especially those using high-dose oral contraceptives) are at increased risk of developing inflammation of the veins (phlebitis), which can lead to clots in the lungs (pulmonary embolism). This risk increases if the woman smokes. Studies of postmenopausal women on hormone replacement therapy suggest that they face a similar risk. In our opinion, women with a previous history of phlebitis should not use hormone replacement therapy.

Contraindications to Hormone Replacement Therapy

Women with the following risk factors should not use hormone replacement therapy (definite contraindications):

- A history of breast cancer
- A history of endometrial cancer

- A history of pulmonary embolus or thrombophlebitis, severe liver disease, or gallbladder disease
- Unexplained vaginal bleeding

Women with the following conditions should carefully weigh the pros and cons of hormone replacement therapy (possible contraindications):

- High blood pressure
- Migraine headaches
- Gallbladder disease
- Diabetes
- Epilepsy
- Uterine fibroids
- Endometriosis
- Benign breast disease

Side Effects of
Hormone Replacement Therapy

We are quite familiar with the immediate effects of hormone therapy. Though side effects vary from woman to woman, the following are the most common.

Withdrawal periods. The original premise of hormone replacement therapy was that women would feel most normal when they had a normal menstrual cycle. So hormone therapy was designed to produce a bleed that mimics a true menstrual cycle. Ironically, bleeding is a major reason that women reject hormones. Most women look forward to the end of menstruation—the idea of having a period into their sixties or seventies is not appealing. For this reason, the pharmaceutical companies are searching for methods to provide hormone therapy without bleeding. On the sequential method, withdrawal bleeding does not last as long as a natural period, and in some women it eventually stops. But more than 50 percent of women continue to have withdrawal bleeding as long as the hormones are continued. Pain, however, rarely accompanies the bleeding.

Breakthrough bleeding and spotting should not occur on the sequential regimen; if it does, a woman should promptly report this to her physician. However, breakthrough bleeding is a particular problem with the continuous hormone regimen. Bleeding is worrisome because of the possibility that an underlying disease might be present. When this so-called "abnormal" bleeding occurs, many physicians biopsy the uterine lining to check it out.

PMS-like symptoms. An unpleasant side effect of the combined therapies is a PMS-like syndrome consisting of depression, irritability, bloating, and breast tenderness. These side effects are caused by the progesterone component of the treatment. Estrogen can also cause fluid retention and bloating, as well as swollen, sore breasts. Headaches often occur because of increased fluid retention. Some women complain of leg cramps, an increase in vaginal discharge, and a return of acnelike skin problems.

Stomach upset. Estrogen can also cause nausea and vomiting.

Weight gain. Estrogen leads to weight gain in some women. About 25 percent of women taking hormones put on a couple of pounds.

Skin irritation. The transdermal skin patches can cause itchiness and an allergic reaction. The vaginal creams are also occasionally allergenic, as well as messy.

Evaluating Your Symptoms

Before considering hormone replacement, your physician must decide whether your symptoms are actually due to menopause. There are a variety of tests for diagnosing menopause. The gold standard, however, is the measurement of the FSH levels in the blood. Menopause has not occurred unless these levels are elevated, usually above 40 MIU/ml. Doctors conduct this test once a woman has stopped her periods. But the mere presence of an elevated FSH level does not indicate which women need treatment. Some physicians advocate the use of a vaginal smear— somewhat like a Pap smear—which measures the percentage of cells in the vagina showing adequate estrogenic stimulation. If less than 10 percent of the vaginal cells show a good estrogenic effect, the patient is said to have an estrogen deficiency. Unfortunately, results of this vaginal smear are quite variable, so by itself, the smear is not an accurate guide for the need for treatment.

Many middle-aged women display multiple symptoms, all of which tend to be attributed to menopause. But in some women, complex emotional factors rather than physical problems can account for some of these symptoms. It is easy for a physician to simply prescribe hormones, but it is more important that he or she gets to the source of a woman's problems.

Sometimes, a vague group of symptoms occurring in younger women are attributed to an early menopause. Women complaining of nervousness, insomnia, and loss of libido are dismissed as menopausal, especially if they are over forty. If anything, such symptoms may indicate the exact opposite of menopause: PMS. A woman can develop PMS at any time from menarche to the climacteric; premenstrual tension becomes even more common in the thirties or forties. A generally safe standard is that any woman menstruating fairly regularly is not menopausal and will not require estrogen treatment. (It is also rare to have severe hot flashes in the presence of normal menstrual cycles. Such symptoms could be a manifestation of stress or anxiety.)

Complaints of fatigue, insomnia, and weight gain can be associated with an underactive thyroid, so it is important to have the thyroid function checked if one is experiencing these symptoms. Bouts of depression, tension, and anxiety, too, may be completely unrelated to the menopause—psychotropic drugs and psychotherapy may be indicated for these problems.

Estrogens will relieve vasomotor symptoms such as hot flashes, as well as vaginal burning and itching and the accompanying sexual discomfort due to vaginal atrophy. The lining of the urinary bladder and urethra are also estrogen sensitive and dependent; frequent urination and a burning feeling during urination are occasionally due to lack of estrogen and may be eliminated by hormone treatment. However, these symptoms can also stem from a urinary tract infection, which should be ruled out by your physician.

It is important to remember that the climacteric and menopause are natural processes, rather than diseases. They cannot be avoided, need not be avoided, and certainly need not be dreaded. The reassurance that comes from this knowledge will go a long way toward relieving the anxiety some women experience as they approach this stage of life. Also, keep in mind that some menopausal symptoms are temporary and self-limited. They will not persist indefinitely. Some women will have severe symptoms that necessitate treatment; others will not. For those who do, hormones may be a part of that treatment, but are not the only answer. We discuss alternative treatments in chapter 10.

Principles of Treatment

In order to understand the treatment of menopause, recall the basic tenets and implications of the physiologic process:

1. The climacteric period precedes menopause and is a relatively slow process wherein estrogen levels slowly decrease but do not reach menopausal levels.
2. Postmenopausal women still make estrogen in varying amounts.
3. Estrogen does not prevent the aging process, which is determined by genetics and physiology.
4. The only symptoms that consistently disappear with hormone replacement are vasomotor symptoms such as hot flashes and sweats, and vaginal dryness due to thinning of the vagina.
5. The effect of hormone replacement on other symptoms, such as irritability, insomnia, and emotional lability, varies from person to person, depending on the underlying cause of the symptoms and the makeup of the individual.
6. The beneficial effects of hormone replacement have to be weighed against the possible harmful effects, based on current research.
7. Women who have coronary heart disease or who are at increased risk for heart attacks are likely to benefit from hormone replacement therapy. But it is an oversimplification to believe that a pill is enough to change one's risk. Lifestyle changes need to occur as well.
8. Women who have had a hysterectomy are more likely to benefit from hormone replacement therapy with respect to heart disease, since there is no reason to add progesterone. If the uterus is present, progesterone should also be used, unless periodic uterine sampling is done.

9. Women who are at high risk for osteoporosis will also benefit from hormone replacement therapy. However, hormone replacement cannot take the place of exercise and diet.
10. In women who are at increased risk for breast cancer, hormone replacement may be dangerous, as several studies have suggested a link between long-term estrogen use and breast cancer.
11. The greatest preventive health benefits are most likely to be achieved with long-term use (ten to twenty years), but cancer risks also increase with duration of use.

Each woman must decide whether hormone replacement is right for her by weighing the benefits of treatment against the potential risks. To help you make an informed decision, we include table 3, a summary of the risks and benefits of hormone replacement therapy, published by the American College of Physicians in 1992.

Ongoing Research

To determine the safety and effectiveness of long-term hormone replacement therapy, well-designed prospective studies would have to follow large numbers of women taking hormones for a long period of time. Two such studies, funded by the National Institutes of Health, are currently underway. In the so-called PEPI (Postmenopausal Estrogen-Progesterone Intervention Program) study, researchers are following women being treated with estrogen, combined estrogen-progesterone, or placebo, to assess the hormones' effects on bone density, blood lipids, and cardiovascular risk factors. The massive Women's Health Initiative is evaluating all of the risks and benefits of hormone replacement, dietary modification, and supplementation with vitamin

(continued on page 90)

TABLE 3
American College of Physicians Guidelines
Summary of Potential Benefits and Risks of Hormone Therapy

THERAPEUTIC REGIMEN

OUTCOME (Benefits and Risks)	Unopposed Estrogen	Estrogen/Progesterone
Potential Benefits:		
Decreased lifetime probability of developing heart disease	There is extensive and consistent evidence that therapy reduces the risk for coronary heart disease. The magnitude of the risk reduction is estimated to be about 35 percent.	Combination therapy may also reduce the risk for coronary heart disease, but data are not sufficient at this time to estimate the magnitude of the risk reduction.
Decreased lifetime probability of incurring an osteoporotic fracture	There is limited but consistent evidence that therapy reduces the risk for hip fractures. Magnitude of risk reduction is estimated to be about 25 percent. Therapy also reduces the risk for vertebral fractures by at least 50 percent.	Combination therapy as well as unopposed estrogen probably protects against osteoporotic fractures, although the evidence to support this assumption is limited.

TABLE 3 (continued)
American College of Physicians Guidelines
Summary of Potential Benefits and Risks of Hormone Therapy

OUTCOME

THERAPEUTIC REGIMEN

(Benefits and Risks)	Unopposed Estrogen	Estrogen/Progesterone
Potential Benefits:		
Increased life expectancy	By reducing the lifetime probability of coronary heart disease and osteoporotic fractures, therapy will generally increase life expectancy.	By reducing the lifetime probability of coronary heart disease and osteoporotic fractures, combination therapy may increase life expectancy, although possibly not as much as unopposed estrogen therapy. If combination therapy does not provide as much protection against coronary heart disease as does unopposed estrogen, then women at high risk for breast cancer could actually have a decreased life expectancy.

Potential Risks:

Increased lifetime probability of developing endometrial cancer	The evidence is extensive and consistent that therapy increases the risk for endometrial cancer. Risk increases with duration of estrogen use and is about eightfold for 10 to 20 years of use. The risk for death from endometrial cancer is probably not as dramatically elevated because endometrial cancer is generally curable, particularly in estrogen users.	Clinical and epidemiological data suggest that the risk for endometrial cancer is not increased in women taking long-term combination therapy. Prevention of the increased risk for endometrial cancer associated with unopposed estrogen therapy is the only rationale for adding progesterone to estrogen therapy.
Increased lifetime probability of developing breast cancer	The evidence is extensive but inconsistent concerning the risk for breast cancer in women taking unopposed estrogen. The risk for breast cancer is probably not increased among women who take estrogen for a short time (less than 5 years). The risk for breast cancer may increase (about 25 percent) among women who take estrogen for 10 to 20 years.	The evidence is limited and inconsistent concerning the effect of combination therapy on the risk for breast cancer. As with estrogen therapy, there may be about a 25 percent increase in breast cancer risk associated with long-term combination hormone use, but there is concern that the increase in risk could be larger.

TABLE 3 (continued)

American College of Physicians Guidelines
Summary of Potential Benefits and Risks of Hormone Therapy

OUTCOME	THERAPEUTIC REGIMEN	
(Benefits and Risks)	*Unopposed Estrogen*	*Estrogen/Progesterone*
Potential Risks:		
Side effects and vaginal bleeding	About 5 to 10 percent of women will experience symptoms such as bloating, headache, and breast tenderness. However, in most women these symptoms are mild and do not require discontinuation of therapy. Side effects, especially breast tenderness, often improve after a few months on therapy. In women with a uterus, therapy causes unpredictable uterine bleeding in 35 to 40 percent of treated women per year.	The addition of progesterone to estrogen therapy may cause symptoms such as bloating, weight gain, irritability, and depression. In most women these symptoms are mild and do not require discontinuation of therapy. These symptoms are dose related and will generally improve if the dose of progesterone is lowered. Unpredictable endometrial bleeding will occur in 30 to 50 percent of women taking continuous estrogen and progesterone during the first 6 to 8 months of therapy. This bleeding is generally light and stops permanently in most women when uterine atrophy develops after 6 to 8 months of therapy.

Increased need for endometrial monitoring for endometrial cancer in women with a uterus	Women should undergo diagnostic endometrial evaluation if uterine bleeding occurs and no recent endometrial evaluation has been done. If bleeding does not occur, screening endometrial evaluation should be done, probably every year. The optimal interval for endometrial evaluation, however, has not been assessed.	Women who take estrogen plus progesterone do not require baseline or routine endometrial evaluation. Women using cyclic estrogen plus progesterone therapy should undergo endometrial evaluation if bleeding occurs outside the expected time of withdrawal bleeding (days five to fifteen of the month if the progesterone is given on days one to ten of the month). Women using continuous estrogen plus progesterone therapy require endometrial evaluation if they report heavy (heavier than the woman's normal menstrual period), prolonged (more than 10 days at a time), or frequent (more often than monthly) bleeding or bleeding that persists beyond the first 6 months of therapy.
Increased probability of need for a hysterectomy	Women with a uterus have approximately a 20 percent lifetime probability of having a hysterectomy because of endometrial hyperplasia or cancer due to therapy.	Women treated with combination therapy are not at increased risk for hysterectomy.

D and calcium with regard to the overall health of post-menopausal women ages fifty to seventy. In view of the multiple links among diet, estrogen, calcium intake, heart disease, cancer, and mortality, it is most appropriate to undertake this complex, interlocking clinical trial, which is expected to answer many remaining questions about the risks and benefits of these various interventions.

Recommendations
Who Should Take Hormones?

We believe that hormone therapy may be useful for women who have had their ovaries removed before age forty-eight, women who experience extreme menopausal discomforts, and women who are at high risk of fractures or heart disease.

We believe that it is not yet appropriate for every woman to take estrogen just to *prevent* cardiovascular disease. We also do not think it is appropriate to encourage hormone use in those women who have experienced or are experiencing a natural menopause without severe discomforts, and who are at otherwise low risk for osteoporosis.

You and your physician should evaluate whether or not hormone therapy is right for you. Using figure 7, a decision tree on managing menopause, may be helpful. Only you can ultimately decide whether the potential gains offset the risks.

What Should You Take?

If a woman has had her uterus removed, estrogen alone can be used as there is no danger of endometrial cancer. We advise women who still have their uterus to take estrogen and a progesterone. This combination has advantages and disadvantages. Women using combined hormones are less likely to get endometrial cancer, but might be more prone to develop heart disease.

Some women may feel more comfortable using estrogen alone than combined hormones, because so much less is known about the latter. The risk of endometrial cancer increases the

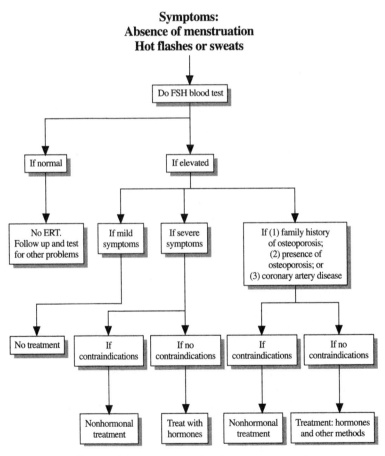

FIGURE 7 *Decision tree for the treatment and management of menopause*

longer estrogen is taken. With this in mind, if you want to use estrogen temporarily to manage menopausal discomforts, unopposed estrogen is a possibility. Women at high risk for osteoporosis
who plan to take estrogen for several years should add a progesterone to reduce the possibility of endometrial cancer and enhance the protection against osteoporosis. If hormone therapy
is used specifically to protect against osteoporosis, we recommend reassessing the need for treatment at age sixty-five.

What Type of Medical Care Will You Require?

Whether you are on unopposed estrogen or combined hormone
therapy, you should be followed very closely by your physician. If
you decide you want to stop taking hormones, taper down the
dosage gradually over a period of a few months. Ask the following questions before beginning hormone therapy:

1. Why do I want hormone replacement—am I having symptoms?
2. What are the alternatives?
3. What kind of medical evaluation is necessary prior to the use
   of therapy?
4. Do I have any of the contraindications to hormone replacement?
5. Have I tried natural ways of coping with menopause?
6. What is the expected duration of treatment? Is the dose as
   low as possible? If I am taking estrogen for a surgically in-
   duced menopause, will the dosage be decreased to mimic
   natural menopause as I grow older?
7. If I take therapy, what medical tests do I need, and how often does my practitioner need to see me?
8. Has my menopause been documented by an FSH blood
   test?

You should also undergo the following tests and procedures before beginning hormone replacement therapy:

- Complete medical and family history with attention to contraindications to hormone therapy
- Blood pressure check
- Breast examination
- Cervical (Pap) smear and pelvic examination
- Annual mammogram
- Careful evaluation of liver and gallbladder function
- Blood lipid tests

A February 1993 article in *The New York Times* summarized a risks-versus-benefits analysis of research on estrogen replacement therapy conducted at Brigham and Women's Hospital in Boston. The analysis, by Dr. Anna N. A. Tosteson, estimated the change in life expectancy of the average fifty-year-old white woman who receives fifteen years of estrogen replacement therapy. (It was not mentioned whether progesterone was included as part of the therapy.) Decrease in the risk of heart disease added about sixty days of life expectancy; decrease in the risk of hip fracture added about twenty-seven days. But increase in the risk of breast cancer subtracted about fifteen days, making the total extra life expectancy on estrogen replacement therapy an estimated seventy-two days.

Of course, this analysis does not address quality of life, but it does seem to diminish the controversy to a matter of about two and a half months rather than a matter of years.

9

Deciding about Hormone Replacement Therapy: Ten Case Histories

The case histories we describe in this chapter are meant to give you an idea of the kind of decision making that is involved in the determination to use hormone replacement therapy, whether in a regimen of unopposed estrogen; sequential combined estrogen-progesterone therapy; or continuous combined therapy. We generally reserve unopposed estrogen for women who have had a hysterectomy. We prescribe continuous therapy for women who do not want to have any more periods.

The women described in the scenarios that follow are composite sketches of patients we have seen over the years—patients who came to us when they suspected they were entering menopause. The names, of course, are fictitious, and the specifics of the cases do not pertain to any one patient; these are just examples to illustrate clinical scenarios. As you will see, many factors influence the decision-making process when it comes to hormone replacement—from the individual patient's experience of menopause to her family history to her concerns about aging.

Sometimes the decision to use hormone replacement does not come until several years after a woman reaches menopause;

in other cases, a woman who has opted to take hormones might change her mind because of new developments in her health. Every woman is different, and hormone replacement is not for everyone. Only you and your physician can decide if—and when—hormone therapy is right for you.

Case 1: Premature Menopause

Joan, age thirty-nine, had had three children by the age of thirty, and had had an intrauterine device (IUD) in place ever since. So when she missed her period for three consecutive months, Joan knew pregnancy was not a likely explanation. After a home pregnancy test came back negative, Joan came in to see us. Joan vaguely recalled that her mother had ceased menstruating in her early forties, and feared that she, too, might be entering menopause at an early age. She did not have many symptoms, though occasionally she awoke in the middle of the night with sweats.

A gynecologic examination revealed that Joan's reproductive organs were normal. A follicle-stimulating hormone (FSH) test, which came back 65, confirmed that Joan was experiencing a premature menopause. There was no family history of breast cancer. We recommended hormone therapy, explaining that her early menopause put her at higher risk for osteoporosis and cardiovascular disease later in life. We also outlined a healthy lifestyle, with dietary and exercise recommendations. She agreed that this was the best course. Still, because Joan had missed only three periods, and some younger women experience a "temporary" menopause, we advised that she take hormones for three months to treat the night sweats, and then stop for six to eight weeks to see if her periods returned. They did not, her FSH remained elevated, and she resumed hormone therapy. She has been symptom-free ever since.

96 The Menopause Book

Case 2: Breast Cancer and Menopause

Though Yvonne, age forty-eight, had missed only two periods, she had been experiencing sleep-disturbing flushes and sweats for almost five months. Her significant medical history included the fact that she had had breast cancer five years earlier. She had undergone a lumpectomy, followed by a course of chemotherapy (her lymph nodes had been negative and the tumor was small) and radiation therapy. Subsequent mammograms and follow-up examinations had been normal.

Yvonne asked us about hormone replacement, complaining that her insomnia was leaving her extremely fatigued. We discussed the pros and cons of hormone treatment, and decided that in view of her history of breast cancer, alternative treatments would be preferable to alleviate her problems. We advised her to begin an exercise regimen, since physical activity helps to reduce hot flashes as well as to prevent chronic diseases. We also prescribed Bellergal-S, a sedative that alleviates hot flashes, to help her sleep during the night.

Yvonne returned to our office six months later. Her hot flashes were under control and were no longer disturbing her sleep.

Case 3: Menopause and a Family History of Osteoporosis

Alice, a fifty-one-year-old lawyer and mother of three, was only mildly surprised when her periods ceased, since many of her peers had already entered menopause. Though Alice occasionally woke at night with sweats, she experienced only mild flushes during the day, and had no other symptoms.

When she had gone six months without menstruating, Alice consulted us. Indeed, her blood FSH levels were elevated, and her menopause was confirmed. Though she was functioning well, and her symptoms were minimal, Alice had a strong family history of osteoporosis. Both her mother and grandmother had suffered hip fractures when they were in their seventies. Alice was thin and fair—additional risk factors for the bone disease—so we conducted a baseline bone density study.

A double photon bone densitometry scan indicated that Alice was already showing a tendency toward mild osteoporosis. We recommended hormone replacement therapy. Alice had no family history of breast cancer, but her father had died of heart disease. She agreed that the benefits of hormone treatment outweighed the potential risks, and took our advice. In addition, she began supplementing her diet with calcium and working out with an exercise trainer three times a week.

Case 4: Symptomatic Menopause

Phoebe was fifty when she suspected she might be menopausal. She had not menstruated for three months, and was waking up every night with severe flushes and sweats. The resulting loss of sleep was making her irritable during the day. Phoebe felt that life with these symptoms was becoming unbearable, and asked us if hormones might be the answer.

A gynecologic examination was essentially normal; not surprisingly, her blood FSH was elevated. Phoebe had recently had a normal mammogram and had no family history of breast cancer. Nor were there any other contraindications to hormone therapy. Together with Phoebe, we decided that hormones would be an appropriate solution. However, because Phoebe was not at high risk for osteoporosis or cardiovascular disease, we told her there was no need for long-term therapy, particularly if she developed a healthy lifestyle, including exercise.

We told her we would keep her on hormone replacement therapy for three to four years, and then gradually wean her off the hormones, so that she would have minimal symptoms upon their withdrawal. She promised to come in for checkups twice a year and to obtain a mammogram once a year. Phoebe's hot flashes disappeared within two weeks of beginning therapy.

Case 5: Symptom-Free Menopause

When Phyllis came in at age fifty-two for her annual checkup, she reported that she had not had a period for about a year. When asked whether she had experienced any unusual symptoms, she said she had no complaints. A legal secretary and mother of three, Phyllis led a busy life. She put aside two hours a week for an exercise class and played tennis on the weekends.

Her examination was completely normal. She had no problems regarding sexual function, and no family history of osteoporosis or cardiovascular disease. Still, many of her friends were taking hormones, and she had heard that hormone use could delay some of the problems associated with aging. She asked about it, and we discussed the pros and cons. In the end, we both agreed there was no need for her to take hormones, though we advised her to continue exercising and to maintain a balanced diet so that she would remain at low risk for osteoporosis and heart disease.

Case 6: Hysterectomy and Menopause

When Abigail, forty-seven, came in for a routine checkup, we discovered a mass in her left ovary. After an appropriate workup, including a sonogram (a test that uses sound waves to show body structures) and blood tests, we operated to remove the mass. We found that she had a benign ovarian cyst, endometriosis (or endometrial tissue outside of the womb) in both ovaries, and uterine fibroids (another type of benign growth).

Abigail had to have a complete hysterectomy, with removal of her uterus and both her ovaries. There were no complications. Since the endometriosis had been treated surgically, we discussed hormone replacement therapy. She began it immediately to avoid the severe symptoms that are usually associated with a sudden surgical menopause. Because her uterus had been removed, we prescribed unopposed estrogen. We advised her to continue the therapy for about four years (then she would be fifty-one, the average age for menopause), at which time we would reevaluate her need for it.

Case 7: Painful Intercourse after Menopause

When Susan became menopausal at fifty-two, she experienced no symptoms. She continued to lead the active life that keeping up with her extended family demanded, and even managed to polish her golf game to the point where she came in second in the local Women's Championship Series. She was tall and thin, but had no history of osteoporosis in her family, and a bone density study had been normal. Susan did not consider hormone replacement therapy until four years later, when she began experiencing sexual problems.

When she came back to see us at fifty-six, Susan complained that her vagina had become increasingly dry during intercourse. In fact, sex had become almost impossible because of the pain and tightness that had developed. Examination revealed that her vagina had become atrophic; she even experienced pain during the exam. Because her pain during sex (*dyspareunia*) was so extreme, and lubricants had not been effective, we discussed the use of hormones to treat the problem. There was no family history of breast cancer. After a baseline mammogram indicated that her breasts were normal, we decided to place her on hormone replacement therapy. Her vaginal symptoms disappeared within two months, and she was able to resume a normal sex life.

Case 8: Elective Hormone Therapy

Lois, forty-eight, had been taking oral contraceptives since the birth of her last child eight years earlier. She was having regular periods and feeling fine. When she came in for her annual checkup, we explained that the birth control pill was producing an artificial period, and that as long as she continued taking the pill, there would be no way to know whether she was entering menopause. Once she did become menopausal, of course, birth control would no longer be necessary.

She agreed to stop using the oral contraceptives so that she could see if her periods continued. She came back to see us two months later. She had not had a period, so we tested her blood FSH level and found it to be elevated in the 80s range, consistent with menopause.

Lois experienced no symptoms after going off the birth control pill: no flushes, no sweats, and no painful intercourse. But she had read and been told by many of her friends that hormone replacement therapy was important for her skin and her overall well-being. We gave her the facts about hormones. Though Lois was not at high risk for osteoporosis or atherosclerosis, it was important to her that she have the added protection that estrogen might offer. She also wanted to ensure that she would not develop the vaginal symptoms that could cause sexual problems later on. Based on all she had read, Lois elected to take hormones. We stressed that she would need biannual checkups and annual mammograms.

Case 9: Cardiovascular Disease and Menopause

Anita was fifty-one when she awoke one night with a pain in her chest that radiated down her left arm. Her husband rushed her to the emergency room, where Anita was diagnosed with a heart attack. She was treated in the hospital, and recuperated fully. She was subsequently placed on a stringent low-fat diet, as well as an exercise program designed to condition her heart.

Anita had experienced menopause a year and a half earlier. We had discussed hormones then, but because Anita had no symptoms, we had decided not to institute therapy. Following her heart attack, we reevaluated the situation. Anita had no family history of breast cancer. We also ruled out other contraindications to hormone therapy. In light of her heightened cardiovascular risk, we decided she should start hormone therapy.

Case 10: Breast Cancer after Menopause

Patricia, fifty-five, had been on hormone replacement therapy for five years because of severe menopausal symptoms of vaginal dryness, sweats, and flushes and a family history of osteoporosis. (A bone density study had indicated the need for hormone therapy as well.) The hormones had alleviated her symptoms and, presumably, slowed her bone loss. She had been feeling well.

When she came in for her annual checkup, she told us that

her sister, who was five years younger than her, had just been diagnosed with breast cancer. She related that her mother's sister had also had breast cancer, and said that she realized that this evolving family history placed her at high risk for the disease.

We discussed what is known about the relationship between estrogen and breast cancer (see chapter 13) and decided that we should wean Patricia off the drugs slowly, so that any withdrawal symptoms would be minimized. However, Patricia remained concerned about her risk for osteoporosis. We conducted another bone density study, and found that Patricia did, indeed, have mild osteoporosis. We strongly advised that she begin an exercise program and supplement her diet with calcium and vitamin D. In the future, Patricia may be eligible for tamoxifen to decrease her risk of breast cancer and osteoporosis. However, the study evaluating this is ongoing. She may also be a candidate for the new biphosphonate therapies, once they are fully approved and available.

10

Alternatives to
Hormone Therapy

If you are not a candidate for hormone replacement—or the idea of taking hormones just does not feel right for you—alternative treatments for menopausal problems are also available. Patients with breast cancer, endometrial cancer, and other medical contraindications to hormone replacement may still have risk factors for osteoporosis and cardiovascular disease; they may also suffer from severe menopausal symptoms that require treatment. These patients present a clinical challenge to the practicing physician, but they can be helped.

Certain nonhormonal medications are effective in reducing hot flashes and related symptoms, and others can be used to treat osteoporosis and help prevent cardiovascular disease. But certain lifestyle changes—namely, diet and exercise—can also go a long way in terms of disease prevention. This chapter covers two treatment areas: lifestyle measures and alternative medications. (Although we briefly discuss the role of exercise and diet in treating menopausal symptoms in this chapter, the following two chapters offer more detailed advice on nutrition and exercise after menopause.)

Exercise

There is increasing evidence that physical activity and physical fitness decrease the risk of a number of common diseases, including coronary heart disease, osteoporosis, cancer, and depression. Although most of the studies demonstrating the role of exercise in disease prevention have been done in men, at least one study in women has shown that the more physically fit women are, the less likely they are to experience complications from several chronic diseases. In fact, regular exercise results in a decrease in mortality among women from all causes.

In women who are not on hormone replacement, exercise is particularly crucial in preventing heart disease and osteoporosis, but all women can benefit from regular physical activity. Exercise has even been shown to reduce hot flashes.

Exercise and Heart Disease

Regular exercise works to reduce several risk factors for heart disease, including high blood pressure, diabetes, obesity, and high cholesterol. It may also help create healthier patterns in your lipoproteins, the carriers of fat and cholesterol in the blood. Exercise has a beneficial effect on your high-density lipoproteins (HDL), which protect against atherosclerosis, by keeping cholesterol from adhering to the inner walls of the blood vessels. (As we discussed earlier, cholesterol left on blood vessels can form plaque that narrows vessels, eventually blocking blood supply to the heart.)

Very active women (for example, long-distance runners) have been shown to have extremely high HDL levels. HDL increases after at least three months of fairly strenuous activity (such as running ten to fifteen miles per week) or after at least four months of more moderate activity (such as walking thirty miles per week).

Exercise and Osteoporosis

Many aerobic exercises that improve cardiovascular fitness are also beneficial in maintaining bone density and preventing osteoporosis. Recent studies have shown that women who engage in active fitness programs that include weight-bearing exercise have higher bone densities than sedentary women. Weight-bearing exercise includes impact aerobics, resistance training, jogging, and other activities that involve the use of large muscle groups to resist counterpressures; in contrast, swimming and casual walking cause only minimal changes in bone density. Stress placed on the bone by muscles during exercise is thought to cause an increase in the activity of bone-forming cells, which results in a buildup of bone density.

Even if a woman is postmenopausal, she can increase her bone density with a moderate exercise program. Studies in postmenopausal women have shown a 35 percent increase in vertebral bone mass after just eight months of moderate aerobic exercise (one hour twice weekly). There are still questions about how long the effects of exercise last and how much activity is necessary to prevent osteoporosis. Until adequate long-term research becomes available, the current opinion is that regular, not occasional, exercise may be necessary to maintain the result.

Hot Flashes

Physical activity can also reduce hot flashes. During exercise, the brain releases chemicals known as endorphins, which are thought to help decrease the flushes. In a recent study, physically active postmenopausal women were much less likely to suffer from moderate and severe hot flashes than their sedentary counterparts.

* * *

Exercise is not a panacea, but together with other appropriate lifestyle and nutritional measures, it can be considered a very useful additive, and in many instances, alternative, to hormone therapy.

Diet

A healthful, balanced diet is also key to preventing heart disease and osteoporosis, not to mention cancer and other chronic diseases. When combined with exercise, a low-fat diet not only helps control weight, it can prolong life. Postmenopausal women have special nutritional needs—whether or not they take hormones, they should be consuming adequate amounts of calcium and vitamin D for bones, and minimal quantities of artery-clogging fat and cholesterol.

Diet and Heart Disease

Many studies have implicated the typical high-fat American diet in the development of high blood pressure and atherosclerosis. Limiting fat intake to no more than 25 to 30 percent of total calories (most Americans consume between 35 and 40 percent) not only helps reduce the chances of getting heart disease, it also helps lose weight. The reason: fat has more than twice as many calories per gram as pure protein or carbohydrate. (As we have discussed, obesity is an important heart disease risk factor.)

Paying attention to the *kinds* of fat also pays off in terms of the health of the heart. The saturated fats—those derived from animal products, such as milk, cheese, and meat—do the most damage. They raise the blood cholesterol, lower HDL (or good cholesterol) and raise LDL (or bad cholesterol). The polyunsaturated fats, which include most vegetables oils (for example, corn, sesame, and soybean) and some fish oils, protect against heart disease by decreasing total cholesterol and lowering LDL. (Unfortunately, they also seem to lower HDL.) Monounsaturated fats such as peanut and olive oils also lower LDLs. People should basically eat more polyunsaturated and monounsaturated fat and less saturated fat, while cutting back on the total amount of fat. Carrots, high in beta carotene, may help to decrease cholesterol absorption. (They are also an excellent source of fiber.)

Diet and Osteoporosis

Specific nutritional requirements during menopause include calcium and vitamin D, the nutrients most directly involved in bone maintenance. Calcium-rich foods include dairy products, broccoli, soybeans, and green leafy vegetables like spinach and kale. If you are a postmenopausal woman, you need to consume between 1,000 and 1,500 milligrams of calcium per day in order to maintain an adequate calcium balance. If your calcium intake is less than 1,000 milligrams per day, your body will leach the calcium it needs from your bone. The lower your calcium intake, the more quickly you will lose bone mass.

Unfortunately, dietary surveys indicate that the typical American diet contains only 400 to 500 milligrams of calcium per day—far from adequate. For this reason, calcium supplementation is important in all postmenopausal women. Keep in mind, too, that both caffeine and alcohol increase the loss of calcium through your stool and urine.

All women lose some bone mass, and although a balanced calcium metabolism is important, calcium supplementation alone is not enough to prevent osteoporosis. One study did show, however, that when combined with exercise, a calcium-rich diet could delay the average age of fractures associated with osteoporosis by ten years.

Vitamin D is essential for calcium absorption and utilization. The recommended daily allowance (RDA) for vitamin D is 200 international units (IU) daily for women ages fifty and over; most older women consume less. Many experts feel that the RDA is inadequate and that postmenopausal women should consume at least 400 IU of vitamin D per day. Living in a southern climate and being exposed to the sun a great deal enhance your vitamin D. Other good sources of vitamin D include fish oils, egg yolks, butter, and liver.

Hot Flashes

Both caffeine and alcohol can exacerbate hot flashes. Avoiding caffeinated and alcoholic beverages, or at least keeping consumption to a minimum, may help control these symptoms.

Alternative Medications

Tamoxifen

Tamoxifen, a synthetic hormonelike drug, mimics some of the effects of estrogen in the body, but, unlike estrogen, is not contraindicated for women with breast cancer. In fact, tamoxifen is used to *treat* breast cancer, and has been found to prevent recurrence. In postmenopausal women, the administration of tamoxifen results in lipid changes similar to those caused by estrogen replacement therapy. Researchers have reported a 20 percent decrease in serum cholesterol (a blood lipid discussed in chapter 12)—primarily due to a reduction in LDL—in women who took 20 milligrams of tamoxifen per day for three years. The effect was sustained with continued treatment.

Laboratory studies (using a test-tube bone system) have

also demonstrated that tamoxifen blocks bone loss. In a recent human study, postmenopausal women taking tamoxifen experienced increases in bone mineral density of the spine (16 percent per year), whereas women who were not given the drug lost 1 percent of their bone mass per year. Whether this effect will result in a reduction in fractures remains to be seen.

Though tamoxifen is well tolerated by patients with breast cancer, it tends to cause hot flashes, vaginal discharge, and irregular menses in about 20 to 30 percent of patients. More serious side effects are infrequent at the dose of 20 milligrams per day. (Some women have experienced eye problems following higher doses.) Like estrogen, tamoxifen is also associated with an increased risk of thromboembolic (clotting) disease.

The risk of endometrial cancer associated with tamoxifen therapy is difficult to determine. There are many case reports describing the development of endometrial cancer in patients receiving tamoxifen. But because patients with breast cancer share several risk factors with patients who have endometrial cancer, it is unclear whether the increased incidence is related to the tamoxifen or to the shared risk factors. A study that compared tamoxifen-treated breast cancer patients to breast cancer patients not receiving this treatment found an increased incidence of endometrial cancer in those taking the drug (researchers observed a 1.4 percent increase in risk in those on tamoxifen, compared to a .2 percent increase in the control group). Patients in this study received 40 milligrams per day of tamoxifen, however—more than would normally be given for treatment of menopause. (Incidentally, the longer the duration of therapy, the higher the incidence of endometrial cancer.) In a similar study using 20 milligrams a day, six patients on tamoxifen developed endometrial cancer, compared to none in a control group. Recently, studies have shown an increase in endometrial polyps (benign growths in the lining of the uterus) associated with tamoxifen. Patients taking this drug should be checked by a gynecologist twice per year.

More information on tamoxifen use in postmenopausal women will be forthcoming from a large-scale study of the drug now under way at the National Cancer Institute. The National Surgical Adjuvant Breast Cancer Prevention Trial, which includes 16,000 women at risk for developing breast cancer, will evaluate tamoxifen's cardiovascular benefits, its effects on the endometrium and on bones, and its usefulness in preventing breast cancer. Due for completion in the late nineties, this trial should enable us to better define the role of tamoxifen in the treatment of menopause.

Drugs for Osteoporosis

Calcitonin. A synthetic version of the bone-building hormone calcitonin is the only drug besides estrogen that is approved by the U.S. Food and Drug Administration for the treatment of osteoporosis. Several studies have demonstrated that calcitonin produces a beneficial effect on bone metabolism and bone density within one to three years of initiating treatment.

Calcitonin is expensive and requires intravenous administration, though a nasal spray is currently under investigation. Salmon calcitonin is much more potent than human calcitonin, but its use may produce an allergic reaction, causing the body to attack its own natural calcitonin. Resistance to the drug is reduced by an alternate-day schedule; resistance also seems to decrease when the drug is administered through the nose.

Etidronate. Belonging to a class of drugs known as biphosphonates, etridonate helps to prevent bone resorption by blocking the action of the cells that break down bone (osteoclasts).

In a study of sixty-six osteoporotic postmenopausal women, patients receiving etidronate showed a significant increase in vertebral bone mass, as well as a significant decrease in vertebral abnormalities. However, biphosphonates are not easily absorbed by the body, and may cause gastrointestinal irritation. In addition, the dosage of etidronate that inhibits bone resorption also interferes with calcium deposition, so only short-term, intermittent administration of the drug is feasible at this time.

Sodium fluoride. Sodium fluoride has been shown to increase vertebral bone density in some women, but is not that useful because of troublesome side effects that affect about 20 percent of patients taking it. These side effects include stomach upset, sore joints, and muscle pain. Also, despite sodium fluoride's positive effect on bone mass in the spine, it does not always reduce the incidence of vertebral fractures, and it decreases bone density in the wrists. More clinical studies are needed before sodium fluoride's efficacy can be assessed.

Calcitriol. A byproduct of vitamin D metabolism, calcitriol increases calcium absorption and stimulates the function of osteoblasts, the bone-building cells. Calcitriol is still experimental: studies are currently under way to evaluate its effectiveness and establish proper dosages for use in treating osteoporosis.

Medications for Hot Flashes

Bellergal-S. Bellergal-S is the most commonly used non-hormonal drug for the treatment of hot flashes and other vasomotor symptoms. Because it contains phenobarbital, a sedative, it is useful in patients who suffer from insomnia due to hot flashes. The disadvantage is that, because it contains a sedative, it can also be habit-forming. For this reason, it should only be used on a short-term basis, until the hot flashes stop. We usually prescribe the drug for about six months. In our experience, it helps only a minority of women.

Clonidine. A drug commonly used to treat high blood pressure, clonidine may also help to alleviate hot flashes. For hot flashes, the dose is lower than that used for hypertension.

11
Exercise

Exercise should be a part of every pre- and postmenopausal woman's lifestyle. As we discussed in chapter 10, regular physical activity can alleviate menopausal symptoms, prevent chronic diseases, and help lose weight. Getting in shape can also improve psychological well-being. Regular exercisers feel better about themselves in general. Being active relieves tension, anxiety, and depression. Furthermore, feelings of physical and mental health often encourage us to improve other habits as well—women who exercise are more likely to eat better, sleep more regularly, and cut down on alcohol consumption and drug use.

Components of Fitness

There are many components of physical fitness, each important in its own right. The three that are most significant to postmenopausal women are body composition (how much of the body is fat and how much is lean muscle, bone, and water), flexibility (the degree to which muscles and joints let us bend, stretch, and twist), and cardiovascular or aerobic efficiency (the body's ability to extract oxygen from the air breathed in and speed it via the blood to every cell in the body). Engaging in activities that stress the bones—and thus maintain bone density and strength—is also particularly important after menopause, when osteoporosis risk increases.

Body Composition

Just as bone mass decreases with age, so does muscle mass. As the body loses muscle, its resting metabolism slows down, since fat does not require as many calories to function as more active muscle tissue. Thus, the body needs less fuel, excess calories are stored as fat, and we experience the unfortunate phenomenon known as "middle-age spread."

Without both aerobic exercise to burn off accumulating fat and strengthening activities to keep muscles from atrophying, most adults experience an unhealthy shift in body composition as they age, becoming more fat and less lean. It is a vicious cycle: even without increasing food intake, the more fatty tissue one has, the fewer calories are required, and the more calories are stored as additional fat, the more difficult it becomes to lose weight.

As muscles—and surrounding bones, tendons, and ligaments—deteriorate, one also becomes more prone to injury, not to mention chronic problems like back pain and osteoporosis. A balanced exercise regimen will help to reduce excess fat and preserve lean tissue, producing a wide range of benefits.

Aerobic Capacity

The rate at which one can keep steadily running, walking, or bicycling depends on one's aerobic fitness. Aerobic fitness is the body's ability to take in, transport, and use oxygen. Of all the measures of fitness, aerobic capacity is probably the most important. Unlike flexibility or muscle strength, the ability to endure an exercise—that is, to jog two miles or to bike ten—is linked to some of the most important aspects of overall good health. Aerobic exercise can change your cardiovascular system and decrease your risk of heart disease. But aerobic workouts must be reasonably vigorous—equivalent, say, to at least ten miles of running per week for at least four months—to have a significant effect on your cardiovascular system.

With aerobic fitness, blood pressure tends to go down, the heart learns to work more efficiently, and the heartbeat slows. One way of gauging your fitness level is to measure your resting pulse rate before getting out of bed. Highly trained athletes tend

TABLE 4
Target Heart Rate for Women

AGE (YEARS)	TARGET HEART RATE (BEATS PER MINUTE)	AVERAGE MAXIMUM HEART RATE (BEATS PER MINUTE)
20	120–160	200
25	117–156	195
30	114–152	190
35	111–148	185
40	108–144	180
45	105–140	175
50	102–136	170
55	99–132	165
60	96–128	165
65	93–124	155
70	90–120	150

Note: These target heart rates are for nonpregnant women; pregnant women should consult their physician.

Source: U.S. Department of Health and Human Services

to have resting heart rates of sixty beats per minute or lower; if yours is eighty beats per minute or higher, you are probably not fit (see target heart rates for women in table 4).

Another way to test your aerobic fitness is to measure the time it takes you to walk or run a mile on level ground. You should be able to walk a mile in fifteen minutes. To improve your time, you must train your body to improve its ability to use oxygen.

In order to achieve a training effect, an aerobic workout should last twenty to thirty minutes and be done at least three times a week. Starting out slowly will minimize the risk of injury as your body adapts to the increased activity. Initially, a day off between workouts is a sensible way to minimize stress on joints and ligaments. By gradually increasing your capacity, you may eventually be able to exercise daily. In general, the intensity, duration, and frequency of aerobic exercise should be increased one component at a time. Varying your type of workout will relieve parts of the body from continual stress, and add a welcome change of pace as well.

When exercise is too intense, the body cannot supply the muscles with oxygen fast enough. It makes up the difference with less efficient anaerobic (without oxygen) metabolism. This produces a substance in the muscles called lactic acid. An excess amount of this chemical interferes with your muscles' smooth and efficient functioning, and may cause cramping pain. The idea is to reach a balance, pushing the body only to the point at which lactic acid can be whisked away in the blood as quickly as it is produced. This way, you can continue to exercise—without pain—for extended periods of time.

Exercise should feel pleasurably tiring. If it is just pleasant, you are probably not working hard enough. If it is only tiring, you are working too hard. An hour after finishing your workout, you should feel good: rested, but not exhausted. The "sing-talk method," although not very precise, can be used to measure how hard you are working out. If you cannot talk without gasping for breath while exercising, you have probably exceeded your target zone. If you can sing while exercising, you are probably not pushing hard enough.

Flexibility

Joints and muscles can lose flexibility with age and lack of use, leaving the body stiff and injury prone. Proper stretching can correct these problems and enhance mobility. Flexibility depends on ligaments, muscles, and the bony skeleton. Since flexibility is measured by the movement that occurs at any joint or group of joints, the condition of any of these areas will be a factor in overall flexibility. In most exercise programs, improved flexibility is accomplished through a routine of systematic stretching of the muscles.

You can increase flexibility by moving each joint gently, without bouncing, and then stretching it a bit beyond its current limit. The resulting tension should not be painful. Stretching to increase flexibility in any joint can also loosen stiff muscles.

Disagreement exists over the appropriate time to stretch. Some researchers recommend that it be done before an exercise regimen or athletic activity, whereas others advise stretching afterward. Although some of the most recent evidence appears to favor the latter approach, recognized experts currently recommend that stretching be performed before and after an exercise program. The type of stretching you do depends on the anticipated exercise. Stretching is of most value to those muscles and joints that have just been—or will be—used.

Back problems, which tend to worsen with age, are often caused by tightness in the back, trunk, and back of the thigh muscles. To test your flexibility in these areas, sit on the floor and slowly reach for your toes, keeping your feet flexed so that your toes point toward the ceiling. If there is a gap of more than two to three inches between your fingertips and your toes, your back muscles need to be stretched. Use this test as an exercise, holding the reach for ten to twenty seconds until you feel the tightness in your back and hamstrings ease.

Muscle Strength

To strengthen a muscle, you must subject the muscle to some form of resistance. As a result, the muscle will *hypertrophy*, or enlarge, and thus be capable of greater force or strength. Most exercise programs result in an increase in muscle strength. However, strength is restricted to those muscles that are actively involved in an exercise program. There is very little crossover of training benefits from one set of limbs to another. Since many of the currently popular exercise programs predominantly involve the lower extremities, you will need to engage in a program involving the upper extremities if you wish to develop arm strength.

Evidence is accumulating that individuals who participate in appropriately planned programs involving the upper arms can also develop some cardiovascular fitness. This would require an aerobic component. Most weight-training programs, however, do not accomplish a significant improvement in cardiovascular fitness, even with significant gains in strength. As a result, in order to achieve cardiovascular fitness, you must also engage in an aerobic program.

Coordination and Balance

The more a muscle repeats an activity, the more efficient that muscle becomes. The more a group of muscles (or several groups of muscles) perform an activity, the more efficient the body becomes at that activity. As you perform the same activity repeatedly over a prolonged time period, it becomes almost reflex in nature. Therefore, even if you feel awkward when first embarking on an exercise regimen, your performance will improve greatly as you become better trained.

Similarly, exercises that are designed to improve a specific function (for instance, the ability to serve a tennis ball) and are used repeatedly will improve your ability to perform that function. Any exercise program will improve your overall ability to perform tasks that require similar or related movements. (For example, after several weeks of weight training, you will probably find that it gets easier to carry bags of groceries.) Another benefit to being active is that exercising regularly refines your coordination and balance, making it less likely that you will experience a disabling fall.

Controlling Your Weight with Exercise

It is difficult to lose weight and keep it off using diet alone. The body seems to sense when its owner is dieting, and lowers its metabolic rate. In other words, when one suddenly starts to eat less, the body prepares to wait out a possible famine by slowing down and conserving fuel.

If, instead of cutting calories to tip the fuel and energy balance in favor of weight loss, you increase your body's need for calories through exercise, your metabolic rate will remain stable, and even increase. Therefore, a weight reduction program that combines both exercise and diet is more effective, and results in longer maintenance of weight loss than a program based on either one alone.

Weight loss from exercise is slow, and anyone who starts an exercise program with the objective of achieving rapid weight loss is likely to be disappointed. Depending on the intensity of the exercise, it takes an hour to burn three hundred to six hundred calories. Obviously, the best types of exercise to add to your routine for weight loss are those that expend large amounts of calories. Activities that keep a large percentage of the body's muscles working over an extended period of time—cycling, jogging, skiing, swimming, and aerobic dancing—are your best bets.

Table 5 indicates the average number of calories expended during various types of exercise by an average 132- to 154-pound woman. If you weigh less, you will burn slightly fewer calories; if you weigh more, you will burn slightly more. Keep in mind that the body continues to burn calories even after you have stopped exercising: your heart rate and metabolism remain elevated for about ten to twenty minutes, so the body may utilize an additional fifty to one hundred calories before returning to normal. As conditioning improves, however, this additional calorie expenditure will decline, as less time is required for the body to return to resting levels.

In order to lose one pound of fat, you must expend 3,500 calories. Assuming you have no increase in caloric intake, it will take about five to ten exercise sessions to burn this many calo-

TABLE 5
Average Calories Used in Various Activities

ACTIVITY	AVERAGE CALORIES USED PER HOUR
Driving automobile	120
Doing domestic work	180
Walking	210
Swimming	300
Playing tennis	420
Bicycling	660
Running (10 mph)	900

Note: Numbers apply to average 132- to 154-pound women.

ries. In addition, muscle mass increases in the early phases of exercise. Since muscle is twice the weight of fat, you can lose fat without losing weight. You must understand this concept when exercising for weight loss, or you will become extremely frustrated. A more meaningful measure of your progress is the fit of your clothing. If it is becoming looser without appreciable weight loss, you are losing fat.

Some women attempt to lose weight by dieting strenuously while in an aerobic exercise program. Although this may appear to be an ideal method of weight loss, it should be avoided, because the resulting energy loss will make exercise difficult and may result in a feeling of exhaustion that prohibits further activity. A better method is to establish an exercise habit and then slightly reduce caloric intake; gradually increase that reduction over several weeks or until the sensation of being acutely tired no longer persists beyond two hours after exercise.

Most of us are impatient when setting off on a weight loss plan, but it is important to start up slowly. Joining a health club or exercise class is an excellent way to get through the critical early stage of an exercise plan (as many as 50 percent of women lose their resolve and drop out of exercise programs within the first six months). It takes a long time to lose twenty pounds—perhaps six months, or even a year. But remember, we are talking about one year to shed weight that may have accumulated over a period of many years.

Getting in Shape:
A General Fitness Program

Any successful exercise program will take into consideration your objectives and motivation for getting in shape. The goals of women who exercise vary: many women do it for weight control, whereas others wish to improve their health and feel better. You should evaluate your goals carefully before beginning a specific program, though you can always make necessary adjustments as your goals change.

Aerobic Activities

Any exercise program that requires your body to utilize its oxygen stores for a prolonged period of time will result in an increase in your body's aerobic capacity. As the program continues over time, your capability to perform greater activity increases. Aerobic activities include swimming, running or jogging, walking, skiing (especially cross-country), and aerobic dancing. Activities like racquetball and tennis can accomplish the same goal, but frequent periods of rest within the games diminish their effectiveness. Golf is poor exercise for aerobic conditioning unless it includes rapid, prolonged walking. Team sports such as volleyball and basketball are also effective when they involve prolonged activity.

Swimming is an ideal program for exercising both the upper and lower extremities. It is an excellent aerobic conditioner, and has the added advantage of minimal impact. The water buoyancy can be very helpful for individuals with minor orthopedic problems. Because of its low impact and low risk of fractures, swimming is an activity that is especially well suited for elderly women with heart disease. Since it is not weight bearing and has no effect on bone density, however, it will not help osteoporosis.

The rapid increase in the numbers of women of all ages participating in swimming programs attests to its popularity and ability to satisfy a competitive spirit. Masters swimming programs are designed for individuals wishing to maintain an active fitness program using competitive swimming as a basis. These programs for adults ages nineteen to ninety-five (even over) provide active competition within five-year age groups. (U.S. Masters Swimming may be contacted at Two Peter Avenue, Rutland, MA 01543.)

Bicycling is an enjoyable activity with significant aerobic benefits. While bicycling primarily uses the legs, riding at an active pace will exercise the abdomen, lower back, and parts of the upper body as well. Cross-country skiing and rowing are also effective forms of aerobic exercise.

For most individuals, running, jogging, or walking makes up the primary exercise program. A walking or jogging program has the advantage that it can be done virtually anywhere and in any weather. (Most current aerobic research has been performed on joggers.) A twenty- to thirty-minute jog or forty-five- to sixty-minute walk three to four times a week will enable almost anyone to achieve aerobic fitness.

Circuit training is a recent addition to the aerobic arsenal. Now available in many public parks and recreation areas, circuit training offers running, jumping, climbing, pulling, and pushing exercises at regular intervals. Recommended levels or times are usually posted for each activity. By combining several types of exercise, you can develop both muscular strength and aerobic fitness. A major advantage of circuit training is that the change in activity helps to avoid the boredom of a single program and thus encourages continued participation. If you are interested in increasing strength as well as fitness, circuit training is a good choice.

Indoor exercise machines that imitate outdoor activities offer another alternative. These devices—rowing machines, stationary bicycles, machines that imitate cross-country skiing, treadmills, and stair-climbers—have been used for years in rehabilitation programs, so their aerobic and strength-building benefits are proven. An advantage of using exercise machines is that they allow you to exercise in a secure, protected environment. This becomes very important when inclement weather or personal safety is a factor. Another advantage is that many of the machines have resistance features so that as your conditioning improves, exercising at the same speed requires greater effort.

Some people find this type of exercise program to be boring, though you can keep stimulated by watching television, reading a book, or listening to music while you work out. There is also a safety issue involved in using these machines: they can lead to injury if used improperly. For example, setting a treadmill too fast can result in injuries during attempted dismount; rowing machines used improperly can cause lower back problems. Most exercise equipment comes with advice for use. As long as you use an exercise machine correctly, you can achieve your fitness goals as safely and efficiently as you would following any other program.

A well-rounded exercise program should aim at improving strength and flexibility as well as aerobic capacity. Calisthenics or weight training can be added to strengthen parts of the body neglected by your choice of aerobic exercise. This may include the abdominal and upper-body muscles. You might alternate days of aerobic workouts with days of strength training. Whether done alone or as part of a longer workout, the aerobic segment should begin with a warm-up and be followed by a cool-down to avoid muscle injury.

Activities to Promote Muscle Strength and Toning

Strength training is based on the principle of resistance. A muscle must have a resistance to its action to stimulate it to hypertrophy, or enlarge. This can be accomplished by a number of methods: free weights, isometric exercises, elastic resistance (using exercise bands), body weight resistance (as with push-ups), or weight-training machines. Each of these methods will increase strength. For safety reasons, weight training should always be supervised by a trained instructor. Not only can you hurt yourself if you attempt to do an exercise inappropriately or try to lift too much weight, but you can also strengthen the wrong muscle groups, resulting in an outcome far different from what you were aiming for.

Some women embark on weight training programs for body toning. Though there are now contests for women bodybuilders, participation in such contests is not a common goal. Most women simply want to look better—they want a flatter stomach, smaller hips and thighs, and a firmer upper body. Reducing total body fat enhances appearance further by making muscle definition more noticeable. Some women avoid weight training for fear that they will develop a bulky, masculine physique, but unless they are taking steroids, this is not likely to happen.

Although weight training will increase strength and alter appearance, it is not an efficient method of increasing aerobic fitness. Most weight training programs have only a slight aerobic component. An individual who wishes to develop aerobic fitness as well as strength needs to adopt a general fitness program in addition to weight training.

Prevention of Injury

The most important injury-preventing measures are based on common sense: start gradually, don't overdo it, maintain adequate hydration, avoid high-impact activities, wear appropriate attire, and be aware of your body's response to exercise. (Specific safety guidelines for aerobic, strengthening, and stretching exercises are at the end of this chapter.) It is extremely important to use proper footwear, as the feet are a key component in most exercises. Athletic shoes are designed for specific purposes—running, walking, or aerobics—and unless you buy cross-trainers, they are not transferable. It is best to wear a shoe that is specifically geared toward your form of exercise. A moderately priced shoe will usually suffice, though better-quality footwear may be necessary for strenuous programs and active competition.

During any exercise program, you should be on the alert for warning signs of injury, such as joint pain or persistent muscle ache. If these signs occur, you should stop exercising and modify your program, perhaps by decreasing the length or intensity of exercise. Muscle pain is usually caused by either a buildup of lactic acid in the muscle or damage to the muscle fibers themselves. When exercising for fitness, pain has no place. The adage "no pain, no gain" does not apply to a well-designed exercise program.

For the average woman whose goal is attaining fitness, results can be seen in about twelve to sixteen weeks. You can maintain your new level of fitness without increasing your amount of exercise. The athlete training for a competitive program will require different counseling from that of the woman who is just attempting to get in shape. Athletes need to exercise strenuously over prolonged periods of time to accomplish their goals. They should be encouraged to seek the help of a competent coach for their sport.

Exercise can be overdone. Any activity that is practiced to the extreme can result in injury. Depending on the seriousness of the injury, you could be permanently prevented from exercising in the future. Individuals who are exercising regularly and then experience a prolonged period away from exercise may also find it difficult to start again. On the other hand, your body does require some rest. By paying close attention to your body's cues, you will know when it is time to give yourself a break.

12
Nutrition

Good nutrition is a fundamental part of promoting and maintaining postmenopausal health. Diet plays a crucial role in the prevention of cardiovascular disease and osteoporosis, and may also be linked to breast cancer. What you eat affects virtually every aspect of your well-being. By the time you reach menopause, a lifetime of poor dietary habits can begin to catch up with you.

Obesity is one of the biggest nutritional problems in the United States, especially in the later years. It encourages the development of diabetes, heart disease, arthritis, gout, kidney disease, and certain cancers, and decreases life expectancy. Only 60 percent of obese people reach age sixty, compared to 90 percent of slim people, and a mere 10 percent of obese people reach eighty.

Obesity is the result of an imbalance between the number of calories the body takes in and the number of calories it burns. Overeating and a sedentary lifestyle contribute to this imbalance, leading to fat accumulation. Although obesity can be hormonal (due to thyroid underactivity or hereditary factors), most overweight adults get that way from eating too much and exercising too little.

TABLE 6

Appropriate Weight Ranges for Women 25 and Over, According to Height and Frame

HEIGHT	SMALL FRAME	MEDIUM FRAME	LARGE FRAME
4'10"	96–104	101–113	109–125
4'11"	99–107	104–116	112–128
5'	102–110	107–119	115–131
5'1"	105–113	110–122	118–134
5'2"	108–116	113–126	121–138
5'3"	111–119	116–130	125–142
5'4"	114–123	120–135	129–146
5'5"	118–127	124–139	133–150
5'6"	122–131	128–143	137–154
5'7"	126–135	132–147	141–158
5'8"	130–140	136–151	145–163
5'9"	134–144	140–155	149–168
5'10"	138–148	144–159	153–173

Note: Weights include indoor clothing.

Courtesy Metropolitan Life Insurance Company

Overeating can be triggered by emotional or cultural factors. Children often follow the eating patterns of their parents. Unfortunately, as one ages, one does not even have to increase food intake to gain weight, because the rate at which the body burns energy (metabolic rate) slows down, making it much more difficult to keep weight under control in one's fifties than it was in one's twenties.

As we explained in the previous chapter, one of the reasons for this slowed metabolism is the change in body composition. As one gets older, fatty tissue tends to replace lean tissue (like bones and muscle). Fat burns fewer calories than the same weight of muscle tissue, because it has less function.

What is your optimum body weight? Muscle and skeletal growth is generally completed by age twenty-five. Weight gain that occurs after age twenty-five is usually due to the accumulation of fat. Table 6 can be used as a guide. It shows the appropriate weights for women ages twenty-five and over according to height and frame, in indoor clothing. If you are more than 10 percent above the desired weight for your height and frame, losing weight may boost your health outlook and your self-esteem. (The table should be interpreted with common sense, however. Your individual body type and body composition will influence your weight—there is room for variation.)

Weight Control

As discussed in the previous chapter, exercise is integral to weight control. Table 5 on page 120 compares the calorie-burning potential of various types of activities. If you equate these calories to food (for example, 8 ounces of ice cream equals 300 calories), you can see that exercise alone is not a very quick way to lose weight.

Calorie restriction combined with exercise is the only surefire method of weight reduction. The idea is to reduce the number of calories you consume to the point where fat is no longer deposited in your tissues. Your body is thus forced to draw on some of its own fat stores to meet its energy needs. When your body reaches this stage, you will lose weight. To lose one pound a week, you must consume 500 fewer calories than normal each day. Generally, if you decrease your daily calorie intake by 1,000 a day, you will lose two pounds per week. As you can see, it takes time to lose weight. Not surprisingly, many people become discouraged. To ensure success and to maintain weight loss, you need to modify behavior: you need to adopt a lifelong "portion control" approach to eating.

Weight loss by starvation, on the other hand, is hazardous. Very low-calorie diets should be carried out only with medical supervision. (They can lead to a dangerous condition called *ketosis*, in which fat breakdown leads to the accumulation of hazardous acid products in your blood.) It is also important to ensure that whatever your dietary plan, you consume adequate amounts of the essential minerals and vitamins.

The number of calories required each day to maintain your particular weight is summarized in table 7. You will notice that the caloric requirement decreases with age. This is due in part to the fact that as people get older, they tend to become less active; it is also related to the fact that metabolism becomes more sluggish with age, requiring fewer calories to function.

At the end of this chapter there is a 1,200-calorie diet to work with. It can be varied upward or downward, depending on

TABLE 7
Daily Calories Required by Women to Maintain Weight

BODY WEIGHT (POUNDS)	CALORIC ALLOWANCE		
	22 Years	*45 Years*	*65 Years*
88	1,550	1,450	1,400
99	1,700	1,550	1,450
110	1,800	1,650	1,500
121	1,950	1,800	1,650
128	2,000	1,850	1,700
132	2,050	1,900	1,700
143	2,200	2,000	1,850
154	2,300	2,100	1,950

your individual need. Remember that by reducing your calorie intake by 500 each day, you can lose one pound per week, or fifty-two pounds in one year, in very simple terms. The thinner you are, the more you have to deprive yourself, as a percentage of your total daily intake, to shed those extra pounds. For example, a woman who weighs 154 pounds at age forty-five must reduce her maintenance-level 2,100 calories per day to no more than 1,600 calories per day. A 132-pound woman who normally requires only 1,900 calories per day can eat no more than 1,400 calories per day to reduce her weight.

In summary, prevention of obesity is one of the cornerstones of good health. Weight gain can creep up on a person. If you gain weight, remember that once you lose it, the benefits will be great: you will look better, feel better, and live longer.

General Guidelines for Losing Weight

The following guidelines should help you lose weight.

1. Learn about good nutrition and dieting. There are plenty of books on the subject, but don't be persuaded to go on a fad diet. Avoid any diet that restricts your intake to fewer than 1,000 calories per day. Such a diet won't last.
2. Exercising is an important key to losing weight. Burning calories through exercise goes hand in hand with decreasing your calorie intake.
3. Adopt healthy eating patterns: you want to establish a way of eating that you can follow for a lifetime, rather than just while you are on a diet. Be sensible about your food choices: you do not have to give up the special foods that you like, just eat less of them. Have your favorite dessert once a week, rather than every night.

4. The key to losing weight—and keeping it off—is to do so gradually. It is frustrating to lose only one or two pounds a week, but many experts have shown that gradual weight loss is more likely to lead to permanent weight loss. Also, it is less likely to deplete your body of important nutrients.

A Closer Look at Dietary Components

Changing deeply ingrained eating patterns is not easy. Considering the various aspects of your diet (from fats to fiber) one by one will help you to formulate a prudent dietary plan.

Fats

Although our bodies do require a small amount of fat to function, most Americans consume about 50 percent more fat than they should. Most experts recommend reducing fat intake to no more than 25 to 30 percent of total calories consumed. Keep in mind that you want to choose polyunsaturated and monounsaturated fats over saturated fats, which are more likely to contribute to high cholesterol.

There are a variety of strategies for reducing fat: eat less meat, use skim milk rather than whole milk, steam or poach food rather than frying it, and use margarine instead of butter.

Carbohydrates

In the past, dieting women swore off bread and pasta, but carbohydrates are not as fattening as once thought. In fact, they are only half as caloric as the real dietary villain: fat. At least 60 percent of your daily calories should come from carbohydrates. An important source of energy, carbohydrates are directly converted into sugar, your body's fuel. Choose fiber-rich foods (complex carbohydrates) such as whole grains, breads, pastas, vegetables, fruit, rice, and beans instead of sugar-laden desserts.

Proteins

Proteins should make up no more than 15 percent of your total caloric intake. Most of us eat more protein than is actually need-ed, particularly from animal sources, which tend to be high in unwanted saturated fat. Red meat, which is especially high in fat, should be mostly eliminated. You can substitute fish, chicken, turkey, beans, or egg whites, all of which contain less fat. (Remove the skin from chicken before eating; it is very high in fat.)

Fiber

The part of a plant that you cannot digest is called fiber. Despite the fact that it is just roughage, fiber is an important part of your diet. Fiber promotes bowel regularity, and helps to prevent colon cancer and other intestinal problems such as diverticulosis (ab-normal pouchlike sacs in the colon). It may also lower choles-terol, reducing your risk of heart disease. And because fiber-rich foods are bulky, giving you a satiated feeling, they can even help control your weight.

Vegetables, fresh fruits, and certain grains are rich in fiber. Whole grain products are particularly filling, and therefore help-ful in weight loss. A fiber-rich diet should include plenty of liq-uids to prevent dehydration.

Fluids

Water is important to your body. In fact, two-thirds of your body is made up of this basic fluid. Water transports nutrients and blood products through your circulatory system, helps lubricate your joints, helps eliminate waste in the urine, and facilitates bowel function by softening stool. It also plays an integral part in the body's natural cooling system—the body rids itself of excess heat through perspiration.

Your body requires 2 to 3 quarts of water each day. Half the water we consume comes from food; therefore, at least one quart of liquid should be ingested each day. Fruits and vegetables contain a large amount of water, as does poultry. Six to eight glasses of water are usually recommended each day, in the form of clear water, juices, or low-fat milk. Beverages containing sugar can actually increase your body's need for water by causing an increased loss of fluid through the urine. If you exercise, you need to increase your fluid intake, especially in warm weather when you lose a lot of moisture through sweat.

Vitamins and Minerals

All vitamins and minerals are essential for good health. Vitamins are important for healthy skin and general well-being. A multivitamin supplement containing recommended daily allowance (RDA) levels of the basic vitamins and minerals is very simple to take, and is probably a prudent course if you are not sure that you are ingesting a well-balanced diet.

All *perimenopausal* (around the menopause) and postmenopausal women could also probably benefit from additional calcium and vitamin D supplementation. We recommend taking 1,000 milligrams of calcium citrate during the course of a day—500 in the morning and 500 at night. Your calcium pill must dissolve quickly in the stomach to be absorbed. You can check your brand by placing it in white vinegar (which is acid, like the stomach juices); it should dissolve in thirty minutes. Vitamin D plays a crucial role in the absorption of calcium and the maintenance of a good calcium balance. Approximately 400 international units (IU) per day is a good amount to take, especially if you live in a northern climate and are not exposed to a great deal of sunlight.

Another nutrient that is commonly underrepresented in women's diets is iron, which is required to maintain sufficient levels of hemoglobin (a substance that carries oxygen throughout the body) in the blood. Lack of iron leads to anemia. Women who have increased perimenopausal bleeding are at risk for anemia. Be sure to consume adequate amounts of iron-rich foods; which include dried fruits, beef, liver, soybeans, and spinach.

Caffeine

Caffeine, which is found in chocolate, coffee, tea, some colas, and some pain relievers, is a powerful stimulant to the body and brain. Overconsumption can lead to increased anxiety, and can exacerbate hot flashes. Some women become physically and psychologically dependent on caffeine because of heavy coffee drinking. Withdrawal from caffeine can cause headaches, nausea, drowsiness, and even depression. If you think you may be dependent on caffeine, wean yourself slowly. Decaffeinated coffee is probably your best bet in the long run.

Alcohol

Alcohol should be consumed in moderation, if at all. Remember that alcohol is a source of calories. It also increases appetite and contributes to obesity. A half-ounce shot of whisky, for example, contains 150 calories. If you are a social drinker, you may be surprised to find that 10 percent or more of your daily calories comes from alcohol. You may be able to lose a considerable amount of weight simply by giving up alcohol.

Some studies have shown that a drink a day will increase longevity and prevent heart disease. But while moderate amounts of alcohol seem to raise high-density lipoprotein (HDL) levels, too much may be associated with an increased risk of breast cancer and liver disease. It also makes hot flashes worse. The American Heart Association recommends a maximum of 1 to 2 ounces of alcohol per day.

Specific Dietary Hints
Control Your Weight

Have you ever wondered why there are so many different fad diets, with new ones coming out all the time? The answer is: a diet only works for as long as you are on it. Nine out of ten people regain the pounds they shed as soon as they go off the diet and back to their regular eating habits. So your best bet is to change the way you eat for the rest of your life.

Remember, if you eat *more* calories than your body uses up, your weight will increase because excess calories are converted into body fat. If you eat *fewer* calories than you burn, you will lose weight.

Here are some tips on how to control your weight:

- Keep an honest food diary for two weeks. You will find out exactly what (and how much) you eat. Identifying bad food habits is the first step toward changing them.
- Do not starve yourself. Eat at least three regular meals a day, or divide your nutritional needs into more frequent, smaller meals. This way, you will avoid getting too hungry and "bingeing."
- Keep low-calorie nibbles on hand to cope with hunger pangs and cravings.

- Eat more high-fiber foods. They fill you up, not out.
- Resist that second helping. Your brain needs 20 minutes to register that you are full.
- Consume the majority of your calories during working hours, when you are most active.
- Always read the labels of processed foods and beware of hidden fat and sugar calories.
- Don't chew gum; it stimulates the digestive juices and makes you feel hungry.
- *Cut way down on fat.*

Eat Less Salt (Sodium)

A high-salt diet may contribute to the development of high blood pressure, which, if not controlled, can cause a stroke or heart attack, the leading causes of death and disability in the United States. Blood pressure tends to increase with age. Cut back on salt before you have to. Some people have trouble processing and ridding the body of salt. Too much salt makes your body retain water, leading you to feel heavy or bloated.

Salt is a combination of two mineral substances: sodium and chloride. Just one teaspoon of salt has about 2,000 milligrams of sodium. We only need 1,000 to 3,000 milligrams of sodium each day, from all sources! Most of us eat much more salt than we need. Fast food is loaded with salt, and it is added liberally to many processed foods and beverages. Just take a look at food labels. You will find sodium in soft drinks, luncheon meats, canned and packaged soups, vegetables, frozen dinners, pizza, ketchup, sauces, baked goods, cereals, cheeses, and pickled foods, just to mention a few. Even baking powder and antacids contain a lot of salt. Since most of us also cook and bake with salt and add it to food at the table, it is no wonder we consume too much of it.

Here are some tips on reducing salt:

- Take the salt shaker off the table, do not cook with salt, and start reading labels!
- Avoid salted and smoked foods such as luncheon meat, bacon, hot dogs, smoked fish, and anchovies.
- Avoid salted snack foods, such as pretzels, crackers, nuts, and potato chips. You can buy most of these products without salt.
- Avoid food pickled in salt, such as olives, pickles, or sauerkraut.
- Use alternatives. Reducing salt does not have to mean sacrificing taste. Cook instead with herbs (basil, oregano, rosemary, thyme, dill) and spices (chili powder, curry, cumin, paprika). Use bay leaves for soups, meat, and chicken dishes. Add fresh cilantro or parsley to dips, soups, and stews just before serving. Use lemon juice in vegetables, salads, and marinades.
- Cook potatoes, rice, pasta, cereal, and vegetables in unsalted water.
- If you must use soy sauce, only buy the light kind.
- Rinse canned beans and canned tuna under running water to wash off some of the salt and oil.
- Use garlic and onions (not onion or garlic salt) in your cooking; besides being healthy, they add flavor.

More and more no- and low-salt products are hitting supermarket shelves. Look for them. After a while, you will not like the taste of highly-salted foods.

Cut Down on Sugar

Sugar causes dental cavities and has no nutritional value. It gives your body a quick—but very short—boost, and leaves you craving more. Do not keep sweets in the house. Do not buy grocery products laden with sugar. Take a one-spoon or one-fork taste instead of eating a whole dessert. In recipes, use half the amount of sugar called for. Keep a supply of fresh fruit or canned fruits packed in their own juice.

If food labels mention sucrose, glucose, dextrose, maltose, lactose, fructose, or syrup before the word sugar appears, there is a lot of sugar in the product. (These are all various forms of sugar.) Powdered white sugar, brown sugar, honey, molasses, corn syrup, and maple syrup are all sugar by a different name. Contrary to popular belief, they are not healthier for you than regular sugar.

Artificial sweeteners in tea, coffee, or soda not only give you a craving for sugar, they may also make you hungry. Make your own soft drink with cranberry or orange juice and salt-free club soda, or plain soda with a slice of lemon or lime.

Eat More Fiber

Fiber is found only in plant foods, from cabbage to wheat. Most sources are fat-free and high in nutrients. There are two types of fiber: *Insoluble fiber* cannot be dissolved in water. It is found in wheat bran, whole-grain breads, cereals, vegetable skins, and fruits. It adds bulk to the stool, promotes elimination, and helps prevent constipation and colon cancer. *Soluble fiber* can be dissolved in water. It is found in fruits, vegetables, dried beans, peas, barley, oats, corn, and sweet potatoes. It may help lower cholesterol. Soluble fiber absorbs large amounts of fluids within your digestive system, so drink plenty of water.

Raw fruits and vegetables have more fiber than those that have been turned into juice, peeled, cooked, pureed, or otherwise processed. Uncooked produce also retains more of its natural vitamins.

You need a variety of both types of fiber, but don't go fiber-mad. If you have eaten little of it in the past, add fiber-rich foods to your diet gradually to avoid bloating, cramps, or diarrhea. Choose fiber-rich foods, not fiber supplements that you add to food. Stick to whole-grain breads and cereals rather than processed versions.

Reduce Your Cholesterol

Cholesterol is a fatlike substance that is produced naturally by the body and is derived from foods we eat that are high in saturated fats. Foods of animal origin are particularly high in *saturated fats*— meats, lard, bacon, and dairy products, including whole milk, cheese, butter, and ice cream. Eating too much saturated fat can push your cholesterol to unhealthy levels. (Cholesterol, itself, is also found in certain foods, including egg yolks and shellfish.)

What influences your cholesterol level? You may inherit the tendency for high cholesterol from your parents, in the same way that you inherit the color of your eyes and hair, or your height. Cholesterol levels also tend to rise with age. (A woman in her seventies or eighties, therefore, should not risk malnutrition in an attempt to get her cholesterol down to what it was thirty years earlier.)

Choose protein foods low in cholesterol and saturated fat, such as fish, chicken, egg whites, and tofu. Eat more fruits, vegetables, grains, and beans, which have no cholesterol and almost no fat. Do not cook with lard, butter, shortening, or chicken fat. Use small amounts of soft margarine or cholesterol-free vegetable oils—safflower, corn, sesame, soybean, cotton seed, olive, peanut, and canola. Avoid palm, palm kernel, and coconut oils, which are high in saturated fat.

Here are some tips on low-fat cooking:

- Instead of frying, try grilling, baking, steaming, or roasting. Use a rack to allow fat to drip into a pan. Baste with wine, lemon juice, or orange juice. Do not use fatty drippings. Self-basting birds can be high in saturated fat. Read the label.

- For salad dressing, use half the amount of oil called for and substitute low-fat yogurt for the rest.
- Instead of mayonnaise or sour cream, mix one-third low-fat yogurt with two-thirds low-fat cottage cheese. If possible, use a blender.
- Instead of heavy cream, mix equal parts of low-fat yogurt and low-fat cottage cheese. If possible, use a blender.
- Yogurt will not separate when heated if you add one teaspoon of cornstarch per cup of yogurt.
- In recipes, use skim or 1 percent low-fat milk. Choose cheese made with skim milk.
- Use nonstick pans. Instead of butter, use vegetable oil spray or a little broth, or just brush the pan with oil.
- Do not bake or grill fish with butter; use lemon or a little white wine (avoid cooking wine, which is often salted).
- Cook chili, soups, stews, and spaghetti sauces a day before and refrigerate. Skim off fat collected on top before reheating.
- Marinate with spices, lemon, wine, or tomato juice instead of oil.

Remember, calories found in fat are converted into body fat much more easily than calories derived from other kinds of food.

Eating a Light, Balanced Diet

What is a varied and balanced diet? It is one that combines a wide range of foods from each of the four food groups to make sure you get all the nutrients you need. According to the latest dietary recommendations of the U.S. Department of Agriculture, our diet should consist mostly of complex carbohydrates and fresh fruits and vegetables, with smaller amounts of protein (see figure 8 and table 8). Remember to choose foods low in animal and other fat, cholesterol, salt, and sugar.

Switching from High-Fat Foods to Low-Fat Foods

ice cream	→	ice milk or sorbet
butter	→	small amount of soft margarine
shortening	→	vegetable oil
cream soups	→	clear soups
sour cream dip	→	salsa
potato chips	→	pretzels
iced cake or doughnuts	→	angel food cake
brownies	→	ginger snaps, fig bars, graham crackers
croissants	→	plain bagels
egg noodles	→	pasta
salami	→	extra lean roasted ham or turkey
strawberry shortcake	→	strawberries with low-fat yogurt
oil-packed tuna	→	water-packed tuna
french fries	→	plain baked potato
sour cream topping	→	low-fat cottage cheese and yogurt mixed with some lemon juice

How Much Can You Eat?

The number of servings mentioned in table 8 are only general guidelines. If you want to gain weight, they may not be sufficient; if you want to maintain or reduce your weight, they may be excessive. Nutritional needs for healthy adults can be met with between 1,200 and 3,000 calories a day depending on your

---

Switching from High-Fat Foods to Low-Fat Foods

corn chips	→	plain air-popped popcorn
cheddar cheese	→	part-skim mozzarella
1 whole egg	→	1 or 2 egg whites
mayonnaise on sandwich	→	mustard on sandwich
butter on bread	→	jam only
deviled eggs	→	hard-boiled egg whites filled with tuna or chicken salad
ham and cheese omelet	→	add vegetables to an egg-white omelet
a regular milkshake	→	blend one banana with low-fat yogurt or with 1 cup of cold skim milk
fruit-flavored yogurt	→	low-fat plain yogurt with banana slices or other fresh fruit
bacon	→	lean Canadian or boiled or baked ham
regular french toast	→	french toast made with 1 egg yolk and 2 egg whites. Top with yogurt or fresh fruit

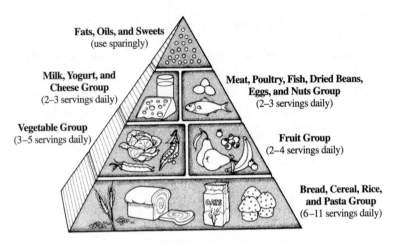

FIGURE 8 *The new food pyramid as proposed by the U.S. Department of Agriculture.*

age, sex, body size, type of job, and level of activity in general. Children, teenagers, pregnant women, and breast-feeding women have different nutritional needs from those of postmenopausal women. Talk to your doctor about how many calories you should consume each day.

Look for a book that lists the caloric and fat content in different foods. It will be an eye-opener. Pick up a cookbook with low-fat, low-calorie recipes to help you eat the healthy way.

Eating Out

Sometimes, the best nutritional intentions can be foiled by a night out at a restaurant. Here is some advice for maintaining healthy eating habits even when you do not control the kitchen:

- Do not be shy about asking how a dish is prepared before ordering.

- Avoid cream soups.
- Avoid deep-fried and breaded foods.
- Ask that meat or fish not be basted with butter or fat during cooking. If that is not possible, do not order it.
- Ask that no salt be added.
- At salad bars, skip mayonnaise-type coleslaw, macaroni or potato salads, bacon bits, and croutons.
- Eat some bread. It fills you up and has few calories. Skip the butter.
- Ask to have any sauces, gravies, salad dressings, or toppings served on the side. Do not pour them onto your food; just dip your fork into them before you eat.
- Ask for a baked potato or a green salad instead of french fries.
- Avoid dishes made with a lot of cheese, such as veal parmesan, quiche lorraine, and some Mexican dishes.
- Order a pizza topped with only vegetables and with half the amount of cheese.

If you have to eat on the run, take along a sandwich made with whole-grain bread, along with a piece of fruit or sliced vegetables. Or bring a homemade muffin, a low-fat yogurt, or some dried fruit mixed with a few nuts. Then you won't be tempted to buy that greasy fast-fried hamburger or fatty hot dog.

Healthful, low-fat brown-bag goodies can include unbuttered popcorn, unsalted pretzels, rice cakes, dry cereal, or bread sticks. For a sweet tooth, pack a few ginger snaps, fig bars, graham crackers, fruit, or carrots. Cook double portions of some food for brown bagging.

TABLE 8
Food Groups to Choose From

MILK PRODUCTS

High in protein, calcium, and Vitamins A and D

Servings Per Day
• Adults: 2–3
• Pregnant and breastfeeding women: 3–4

Foods
• Skim milk, yogurt, buttermilk, cottage cheese (without fat or not more than 1 percent fat).
• Low-fat cheese (not more than 2–6 grams of fat per ounce).

Notes
• Children under 2 need *whole* milk products.
• Parents worried about an older child's obesity or long-term health should not reduce the child's fat intake before talking with a nutritionist or pediatrician.
• Evidence shows that eating foods rich in calcium may help prevent osteoporosis.

MEAT, POULTRY, FISH, SHELLFISH, EGGS

High in protein, vitamin B, iron, and minerals

Servings Per Day
• Adults: 4–6 ounces

Foods
• Lean beef, lamb, veal, pork. Cut off all visible fat before cooking.
• Chicken or turkey. Remove skin and cut off fat before cooking.

Notes
• Organ meats—brains, sweetbreads, heart, kidney, chitterlings, and liver—are high in cholesterol.
• Avoid high-fat luncheon meats, hot dogs, sausages, young bacon.
• Fish is a very good source of low-fat protein. Eat it several times a week. Buy tuna packed in water. Otherwise, rinse off the oil before making tuna salad.

MEAT, POULTRY, FISH, SHELLFISH, EGGS (CONTINUED)

Notes (cont.)
• Shellfish such as shrimp and lobster are higher in cholesterol than most meats. Limit to 1 serving a week.
• Eggs are high in protein. Eat no more than 3 egg yolks a week, counting those in cooking. Egg whites alone are a good source of protein. If your cholesterol level is normal and you depend on eggs for some of your meals, do not stop eating them, unless your doctor says so.
• In order to control your animal fat consumption, substitute cooked dried beans, peas, or lentils for meat several times a week. Or combine them with a smaller serving of meat.

VEGETABLES AND FRUIT

Fresh Vegetables: complex carbohydrates, vitamins, fiber

Servings Per Day
•Adults:1–3

Foods
• Dark green and orange vegetables— especially broccoli, greens, collards, bok choy, kale, brussels sprouts, spinach, or carrots—at least 3 times a week. They fill you up without filling you out!
• All other vegetables. If you buy frozen or canned vegetables, read the labels. Avoid those with creamy sauces, or those high in salt or sugar.

Starchy Vegetables: complex carbohydrates, vitamin B, iron, fiber

Servings Per Day
•Adults:1–3

Foods
• Potatoes are a rich source of nutrients. If you avoid a high-fat topping, they are, contrary to what people think, not fattening.

TABLE 8
Food Groups to Choose From (continued)

Foods (cont.)
• Dried peas and beans: high in protein, complex carbohydrates, fiber, vitamin B, and iron.
• Lentils, kidney beans, pinto beans, navy beans, black-eyed peas, chickpeas (garbanzos)—at least three times a week. They are a good supplement to a smaller meat portion.

Fruit: complex carbohydrates, vitamin C, folic acid, minerals, fiber

Servings Per Day	*Foods*
•Adults: 2–4	• Citrus fruit—oranges, grapefruit, and tangerines—are high in vitamin C. Eat at least one a day. • Cantaloupe, peaches, papaya, watermelon, blueberries, strawberries. All have valuable nutrients. • All other fruits. If you buy canned or frozen fruit, avoid those packed in heavy, sweetened syrup.

GRAIN PRODUCTS

Some protein and complex carbohydrates

Servings Per Day	*Foods*
• Adults and teenagers: 6–11	• Breads, preferably whole grain: rye, *whole* wheat (not just wheat), pumpernickel. Choose enriched products. Also, English muffins, pita bread, rolls, bagels, tortillas (don't fry them). • Cereals, without coconut or coconut oil. Stay away from granola-type cereals; they are high in saturated fat. Read labels for sugar content.

GRAIN PRODUCTS

Foods (cont.)
• Pasta, rice (whole-wheat pasta and brown rice have more fiber).
• For snacks: low-fat crackers, bread sticks, matzos, Rye Krisps, melba toast, low-salt pretzels, air-popped (not oil-popped) popcorn without butter.

HOW MUCH IS ONE SERVING?

Milk Products: One serving = 6–8 ounces of low-fat yogurt, or 8 ounces of low-fat milk, or 1–2 ounces of low-fat cheese

Meat: One serving = about 3 ounces meat or fish—2 slices of lean beef, 3"x3"x¼" thick, or 1 palm-size hamburger patty 3" across and ½" thick

Chicken: One serving = about 3 ounces—1 leg and thigh of medium-sized chicken, or ½ breast

Vegetables: One serving = ½ cup of cooked or 1 cup of raw vegetables, or a small salad

Fruit: One serving = 1 medium orange or apple, or 1 cup of berries, or a quarter of a cantaloupe

Grains, Bread, Cereal: One serving = 1 slice of bread, or 1 ounce of cereal, or ½ cup of pasta, rice, or beans. One whole English muffin, hamburger roll, or hot dog roll counts as 2 servings.

Note: To cut down on eating animal fat, substitute 1 ounce serving of meat with ½ cup of cooked dry beans, peas, or tofu.

Food Labels

The first ingredient listed on a food label is the one most plentiful in the product; the last one listed is least. If one or more types of fat, salt, or sugar are at the top of the label, avoid the product.

Do not be fooled by big letters reading "light" or "lite" on the front of a product—they can mean whatever the manufacturer wants them to mean. The terms have no legal definition. That is why you must still read the label listing the ingredients and nutritional contents. Compare the level of fat to another product.

If a label says "cholesterol-free," beware—the product may still be high in saturated fat. On the other hand, some canned soup and frozen food producers advertise the fact that their products are low in fat and cholesterol, but fail to mention their sky-high salt content.

Many processed products have healthy-sounding names, or say that they are healthy for you. Always use your own judgment. Compare the sugar, salt, fat, and fiber contents of different foods to figure out which food is best for you and your family. Commercially prepared food *can* be a good meal choice, if you select the right brand.

Remember, an informed eater makes healthier choices. Here are some tips on wise shopping:

- Tasty soups and stews can be made with ingredients from a variety of food groups, including lean meat or chicken, vegetables, beans, or potatoes. (For extra no-fat protein, add half a cup of tofu.) With a piece of whole-grain bread, they make a great dinner, lunch, or snack.
- In some parts of the country, the leanest grade of beef is called "select" or "good" and has less fat than "choice" or

"prime." In general, lean cuts of meat are less expensive than the marbled type.

- The amount of fat in beef and pork cuts decreases as you move toward the back of the animal. Chuck, brisket, and ribs have the highest fat and cholesterol content. Tenderloin and sirloin, depending on the amount of marbling, can be moderately high in fat. Eye of round, top round, and flank steak have less fat. Ask your butcher to grind it for you. You will be sure to get the leanest meat that way.
- The leanest cut of pork is loin. Of course, ribs and fat-backs (layer of fatty pork skin) are out.
- Ground turkey can still be fatty because it contains fatty turkey skin. Buy a turkey or chicken breast and ask the butcher to grind it, or do it yourself in a food processor.
- Fresh or cooked vegetables left in the refrigerator too long lose most of their Vitamin C. Frozen vegetables, on the other hand, do not.
- Avocados, olives, and most nuts are high in fat. Eat them in moderation.
- Skim-milk products have as much calcium as whole-milk products.

Making Dietary Changes

Give your system and your taste buds time to get used to your new way of eating. Do not deprive yourself all at once. Start by cutting out high-fat foods. Then progress to limiting the amounts of salt and sugar in your diet. At first, you may miss them, but in time you will enjoy the natural taste of foods. If you backslide for a day or two, do not say "all is lost" and give up. Go right back to eating sensibly. You will feel better, you may prevent illness, and you will probably live longer. Make up your mind today—then make sure your new eating habits are here to stay.

13

Breast Cancer
and Other Breast Diseases

One in nine American women
will develop breast cancer in her lifetime. Two-thirds of those
who do will be over fifty. Breast cancer is a disease of aging; the
risk of getting it increases as one gets older (see figure 9). The
mortality associated with breast cancer also rises with age.

Though the disease is relatively uncommon among women
in their twenties, and only slightly more prevalent among women
in their thirties and forties, the incidence of breast cancer in
younger women has recently been increasing. Some experts attribute the rise to the increased use of mammography, which is
picking up the cancers earlier. One study showed a 29 percent
increase in breast cancer among women ages twenty-five to forty-
four, though only 12 percent of this 29 percent was thought to be
due to mammography detection. Scientists have been searching for other explanations. One theory blames the rising incidence of breast cancer among younger women on the prolonged
use of oral contraceptives containing estrogen and progesterone.

Despite advances in diagnosis and treatment methods, doctors have made little headway in saving women from breast cancer once it is beyond its earliest stages. Because of the failure to
radically improve survival rates, preventing the disease is crucial.

The next best thing, of course, is early detection. Breast cancer is curable when it is found—and treated—early enough.

We do not know what causes breast cancer, but we do know that there are certain risk factors that make it more likely that a woman will get the disease. Though the overall risk of developing breast cancer is one in nine, a woman with no clear risk factors has a significantly lower chance of getting the disease, perhaps one in thirty. Nevertheless, 70 percent of the women who develop breast cancer actually have no risk factors at all. That is why it is so important for all women to be on the alert—having regular physicals, getting annual mammograms after age fifty, and conducting monthly breast self-examinations.

TABLE 9

Women's Risk of Developing Breast Cancer, According to Age

AGE	RISK
25	1 in 19,608
30	1 in 2,525
35	1 in 622
40	1 in 217
45	1 in 93
50	1 in 50
55	1 in 33
60	1 in 24
65	1 in 17
70	1 in 14
75	1 in 11
80	1 in 10
85	1 in 9

Source: 1987–1988 data, Surveillance, Epidemiology, and End Results (SEER) Program of the National Cancer Institute and the American Cancer Society

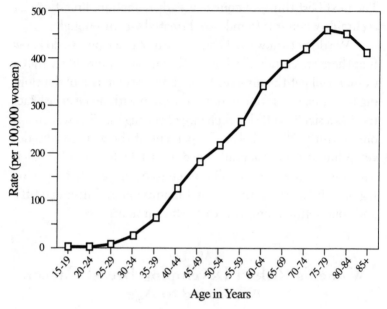

FIGURE 9 *Average rate of breast cancer in women in five-year age groups, 1984–1988.*
Source: National Cancer Institute. Cancer Statistics Review 1973–1988. Bethesda, Maryland: NCI, 1991.

Before we discuss detection and prevention let us take a look at the factors that increase a woman's breast cancer risk.

Risk Factors for Breast Cancer

Family History. There is definitely a genetic component to the development of breast cancer. If you have a first-degree relative (mother, daughter, or sister) who has breast cancer, your risk increases markedly. If that first-degree relative had breast cancer premenopausally, your risk rises even further. A second-degree relative (grandmother, aunt, or cousin) increases your risk slightly.

Pregnancy and Menstrual History. Women who start menstruating early or enter menopause late have a higher risk of developing breast cancer. It seems that the more menstrual periods a woman has during her lifetime, the more at risk she is. In addition, a woman who has her first child before the age of eighteen has half the risk of breast cancer of a woman who has had her first child around thirty. It appears that having a baby fairly soon after starting to menstruate offers some protection. Doctors suspect that the breast may be more sensitive to environmental or dietary factors prior to pregnancy. But while pregnancy seems to offer some protection, women who have their first baby after age thirty-five are at greater risk for breast cancer than women who have no children.

All these factors could be related to estrogen. Perhaps pregnancy interrupts the constant estrogen stimulation to the breast that occurs with repeated menstrual cycles. This theory is borne out to some extent by the fact that women who have had both ovaries removed at a young age have a decreased risk of breast cancer.

Oral Contraceptives. Some studies suggest that the use of oral contraceptives at a young age, for at least five years, may be associated with an increased risk of breast cancer, particularly in women ages forty-five and under. However, breast cancer is very rare in this age group, so the risk for breast cancer from birth control pills is quite low.

Diet. Several studies suggest that a high-fat diet may promote breast cancer, but the data are conflicting. The fact that breast cancer is more common in America and Western Europe than in Japan (an equally industrialized country whose people just happen to consume much less fat) seems to support this finding, though other explanations are possible. Indeed, the risk of breast cancer in Japanese women who migrate to America increases to the American rate within a couple of generations, even if they do not intermarry.

As you know, reducing fat in your diet is important to help prevent coronary heart disease and colon cancer. Although not all researchers agree, reducing your fat intake to 20 percent or less of your total diet may also confer some protection against breast cancer. Researchers do not think that fat directly causes breast cancer, but they believe it may promote malignancy once genetics or other factors initiate it. More studies evaluating diet and breast cancer risk need to be done.

Postmenopausal women who are obese have a higher risk of developing breast cancer. This may be due to a high-fat diet, or it may be that estrogen is produced by fat cells in postmenopausal women, and obese women thereby produce more estrogen. However, *premenopausal* women who are thin have a higher risk of breast cancer than those who are fat. This has never been adequately explained.

Alcohol. Some studies have shown that moderate to heavy drinkers have a higher rate of breast cancer than nondrinkers. Women who are at high risk from a genetic point of view should especially moderate their alcohol consumption.

Radiation. Exposure of the breasts to X rays or other types of radiation at an early age increases a woman's risk of eventually getting breast cancer. Young girls should get chest X rays only when they are absolutely needed.

Estrogen and Breast Cancer

Breast tissue remains dormant until adolescence, when estrogen, progesterone, and related hormones trigger breast growth. The fact that estrogen affects breast cell growth may explain why early menarche and late menopause heighten the risk of developing breast cancer. One interesting study recently compared estrogen levels in thirty-six daughters of young women with breast cancer and thirty-six daughters of healthy young women. The study found that estrogen levels were 27 percent higher in the daughters of those who had breast cancer. This finding has been confirmed by other researchers, and is probably related to the fact that the daughters of the women with cancer also had more regular menstrual cycles.

Other hormones have been implicated in the possible development of breast cancer as well, including progesterone and prolactin (the pituitary hormone that stimulates the production of breast milk). Scientists once believed that progesterone might be protective, because it interrupted prolonged estrogen stimulation to breast cancer cells. But recent studies show that like estrogen, progesterone may produce cell division in breast tissue. Thus, elevated levels of progesterone might also be a negative factor. Prolactin, too, has been shown to stimulate breast cell division.

Because of the well-documented effect that estrogen has on breast tissue, the safety of oral contraceptives and hormone replacement therapy have come into question. We still do not have all the answers, but following is what we know so far.

Oral Contraceptives

The birth control pill has been widely used since the early 1960s. By 1980, more than eighty million women throughout the world had taken oral contraceptives at some time. The relationship between the risk of breast cancer and oral contraceptive use has been well studied. Most studies show that oral contraceptives do not increase the overall risk of breast cancer, but a few studies suggest that certain subgroups of women using birth control pills may be at increased risk.

Five studies reported that oral contraceptive use around menopause was associated with an increase in breast cancer, and one study found that the use of birth control pills in the late adolescent period also heightened breast cancer risk. Several other studies have suggested that oral contraceptive use may increase the risk of getting breast cancer at a younger age. The theory behind all of these findings is that birth control pills may increase breast cell activity to abnormal levels. However, because other studies have yielded conflicting findings, most experts agree that more research is needed.

Hormone Replacement Therapy

The possible link between hormone replacement therapy and breast cancer is the source of most of the controversy surrounding hormone use in postmenopausal women. It seems that long-term therapy, administered in moderately high doses, does carry with it a sizable increase in breast cancer risk, while smaller doses, given for a short period, do not markedly increase risk. The effects of very small doses administered over long periods of time have not yet been studied. Basically, the greater the amount of estrogen taken, the higher the increase in breast cancer risk, according to most studies.

One recent study concluded that women who took .625 milligrams of a conjugated estrogen like Premarin for fifteen years, beginning at menopause, would have a 66 percent increase in breast cancer risk by age sixty-five. Based on most studies, the lifetime probability of developing breast cancer after long-term, high-dose estrogen use is about one to one and a half times greater than average. This is a marked increase, and will clearly have an effect on breast cancer incidence. But the implications of this data for long-term estrogen use have to be weighed in the context of the other risks and benefits of hormone replacement therapy.

The caveat to the studies: their subjects all took unopposed estrogen. Now that we commonly add progesterone to prevent the development of endometrial cancer, these studies are no longer applicable. However, since progesterone may also increase cell division in breast tissue, there is a possibility that combined therapy might also heighten breast cancer risk.

It is also likely that some subgroups of women may be more susceptible to the hormones' effects on breast tissue. Estrogen appears to present a greater risk, for example, to women who have a significant family history of breast cancer.

Mammography

In 1990 in the United States, 150,000 women were diagnosed with breast cancer, and 44,000 women died of the disease. At any one time, nearly one million women will have breast cancer; every hour, about seventeen more women will be diagnosed, and five women will die of the disease. As of now, the best hope of decreasing mortality is early detection. The rationale for mammography is that it detects breast cancer in its asymptomatic stage—before it can be seen or felt by you or your physician. Mammography can give you up to a two-year head start on breast cancer treatment.

It has been estimated that if all women followed recommended guidelines for mammography, breast cancer mortality could be reduced by anywhere from 35 to 50 percent, because early breast cancer is a curable disease. About 90 percent of women with early breast cancer can be cured. The National Cancer Institute and American College of Obstetricians and Gynecologists recommend mammograms every one to two years between the ages of forty and forty-nine and annually after fifty. A baseline mammogram between the ages of thirty-five and forty is also recommended for high-risk women.

The use of mammography has been increasing, but has not yet become a habit for most women. About 66 percent of women over fifty who were surveyed in 1990 said that they had had a mammogram, but less than one-third were getting mammograms on a regular basis. Older women tend to do it less often than their younger counterparts, because they do not appreciate the fact that breast cancer is a disease of aging. Younger women tend to read more, and are more influenced by the media. Some women are also concerned about the theoretical risk of radiation associated with mammography, but there is no need to be. New mammography equipment has reduced radiation to a minimum. However, women under thirty-five who are not at hereditary risk should avoid X rays unless clinically indicated.

Most women understand that a mammogram is an X ray of the breast that is taken when the breast is flattened between two plates. The resulting image is read by a radiologist who has had special training in interpreting such films. Mammography does not prevent cancer, but can pick up tiny cancers that are not palpable. Other methods of early detection include self-examination of the breasts and regular physical exams by a health professional.

Since up to 10 percent of breast cancers are not detectable by mammograms, it is important to have annual breast examinations. Women who have a family history of breast cancer should have biannual examinations. And because a surprisingly large number of breast tumors are actually detected by the patient herself, we cannot overemphasize the importance of self-examination.

Breast Self-Examination

If you regularly examine your breasts, you will detect lesions that are smaller in size than if you waited for an annual or semiannual physical examination by your health care provider. You should examine your breasts every month after your period. Figure 10 illustrates the most commonly used technique for routine self-examination of the breast.

There are several steps involved in the careful performance of self-examination. Visual inspection of your breasts in a mirror should always be followed by careful palpation of the breast tissue. The most important aspect of self-examination is to become familiar with the normal size, general contour, and consistency of your breasts. These factors vary tremendously from woman to woman, but should not vary significantly for the same woman from one month to the next, assuming that she is not on hormones and is not pregnant. (Though there may be slight monthly variations in the breasts of these women, it is still important that they, too, continue to examine their breasts.)

The initial step in self-examination is to observe your breasts while standing in front of a mirror, first with your arms at your sides and then with your arms up over your head. In this way, it is possible to identify any changes in the general outline or size of the breasts, and also to look for any abnormalities in the skin surface. A malignant lump directly under the skin tends to produce a distortion of the breast contour, either by puckering or by dimpling the overlying skin. In certain instances, this may not be apparent when the arms are held at your sides. Stretching

1. Lie down. Put one hand behind your head. With the other hand, fingers flattened, gently feel your breast. Press ever so lightly. Now examine the other breast.

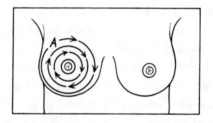

2. How to check each breast: begin where you see the *A* and follow the arrows, feeling gently for a lump or thickening. Remember to feel all parts of each breast.

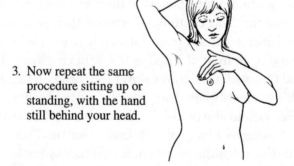

3. Now repeat the same procedure sitting up or standing, with the hand still behind your head.

FIGURE 10 *The three simple steps of manual breast self-examination.*

your arms over your head puts tension on the skin, thus enabling you to notice such changes.

There are two steps to manual examination. First, you should gently press the area around the nipple to see if there is any secretion. The second step, which should be carried out lying down, involves the careful palpation of both breasts. You should systematically cover all areas of the breasts to see if they contain any lumps or areas of thickening.

There are several different techniques suggested for examination; we will describe the most common. Start with your left breast. Put a pillow under your left shoulder and place your left hand behind your head. The fingers of your right hand should be closed together, and your entire hand should be flat during the examination. Press the flat of your hand gently against the breast, and move it in a small, circular motion.

The upper and inner quadrant of the breast is usually examined first, starting from the mid-line over the sternum, or breastbone, and then moving toward the nipple. The area around the nipple should also be palpated at this time. Examine the lower and inner segments of the breast in the same manner. Bring your left arm down to your side, and examine your left armpit, moving the right hand in the same circular motion. Examine the upper and outer quadrants next, starting at the nipple area and moving outward toward your arm. Finish by palpating the outer and lower portion of the breast, starting from the outer portion near your arm and moving inward toward your nipple.

At this point, shift the pillow to under your right shoulder, place your right hand behind your head, and use your left hand to palpate your right breast in the same manner.

Many women are not aware of how lumpy normal breast tissue is. Breasts are made up of many ducts and lobules, and therefore are not smooth and homogeneous. Once you know what "normal" is for your breasts, you are in a much better position to detect an abnormality, should one appear. Do not panic if you do feel something: there are many benign breast conditions, ranging from multiple small nodules in *chronic cystic mastitis* (fibrocystic breast disease) to single large cysts and harmless tumors. In fact, there are approximately four benign lesions found for every malignant one. Even for doctors, however, it is very difficult to judge simply by palpation whether a lump in a breast is benign or malignant.

Consult your physician if there is some distinct change in contour on visual examination, particularly if it is accompanied by puckering or dimpling. You should also seek medical attention if discharge can be expressed from the nipple (unless you are nursing) or if you find a lump that is clearly different and distinct from the rest of your breast tissue—especially if such a lump was not present the month before.

It is not safe to assume that because a benign condition has occurred in one breast, that any lump appearing in another area in the same breast—or in the other one—is also benign. Both benign and malignant tumors can occur in the same patient. One cannot ignore even the sixth, seventh, or eighth mass on the assumption that it is benign because all previous lumps have been.

If you feel a lump or notice some other changes since the last examination, there are several important things you should and should not do. The first important thing is not to panic. The chances of any single lump being malignant are far less than the chances of it being a perfectly benign cyst or tumor and therefore not a threat to life or health. Second—and most critical—any lump you find should be promptly reported. Some women are so overcome with fear that they either try to ignore a lump or tell themselves that they will not investigate it because it will probably soon go away by itself. Not reporting lumps, unfortunately, keeps the death rate from breast cancer high among American women.

All of us have known women so paralyzed by the discovery of a breast nodule that they have hidden its presence from their families and their doctors and have even denied its existence to themselves until the cancer has spread so far that any chance of permanent cure has long been lost. Women are occasionally seen by a physician for the first time with a huge, degenerating tumor that has almost totally replaced her breast. In such cases, of course, there is no chance for cure, and there is even little chance of making the remaining days of the woman's life comfortable.

In summary, careful monthly self-examination of the breasts is probably one of the simplest, least expensive, and most effective techniques available for early diagnosis. It has the potential to save thousands of lives, one at a time. Until we find an absolute cure, breast self-examination, physical examination, and mammography remain our best weapons in fighting death and disability from cancer of the breast.

Evaluation of a Palpable Mass

If you find a lump, it will be evaluated by mammography. You may also undergo breast ultrasound, which can often distinguish between a solid mass, which will have to be evaluated further, and a cyst, or fluid-filled sac, which would most likely be benign.

If you have a cyst, your physician will aspirate the fluid by inserting a long, hollow needle into the breast tissue. If the fluid is clear, no further evaluation is needed. If the fluid is not clear, or no fluid is obtained, you will probably require a biopsy. Likewise, if you have a solid mass, or the breast imaging was inconclusive, you will require needle aspiration, needle biopsy (the needle is used to get a sample of breast tissue, which can be analyzed by a pathologist), or an excisional biopsy (a tissue sample is obtained surgically). In some cases, a benign tumor called a *fibroadenoma* can be identified through breast imaging, but women over thirty should still be biopsied.

Similarly, the detection of a nonpalpable lesion or suspicious cluster of *microcalcifications* (calcium deposits) on mammography must also be followed up by a biopsy.

Breast Cancer Treatment

If you are diagnosed with breast cancer, your treatment plan will depend on several factors, including the size of your tumor and whether the cancer has spread to nearby tissue and lymph nodes. The American Joint Committee on Cancer employs a clinical staging system by which treatment programs are planned.

Stage 0. Carcinoma in situ (cancer cells are limited to within the milk ducts.)

Stage I. Tumor 2 cm or less at its greatest dimension. Lymph nodes negative. No distant spread.

Stage IIA. (1) Tumor more than 2 cm but not more than 5 cm at its greatest dimension. Nodes negative. No distant spread. (2) Tumor 2 cm or less at its greatest dimension. Spread to movable same-side axillary lymph node(s). No distant metastasis.

Stage IIB. (1) Tumor more than 2 cm but not more than 5 cm at its greatest dimension. Metastasis to movable same-side axillary lymph node(s). No distant spread. (2) Tumor more than 5 cm at its greatest dimension. No nodes. No distant spread.

Stage IIIA. (1) Tumor up to 5 cm with nodal spread to same side axillary lymph node(s) fixed to one another or to other structures (grave sign). (2) Tumor more than 5 cm in dimension. Spread to movable or fixed same side lymph node(s).

Stage IIIB. (1) Tumor of any size with direct extension into chest wall, or skin edema, ulceration, or satellite skin nodules confined to the same breast or inflammatory carcinoma (grave sign). Spread to movable or fixed axillary lymph nodes. No distant spread. (2) Tumor of any size or extension with spread to same-side internal mammary lymph node(s). No distant spread.

Stage IV. Distant metastasis present (including supraclavicular lymph nodes).

If you have Stage I or II disease, your doctor will probably recommend either a modified radical mastectomy (surgical removal of all the breast tissue, with the pectoral muscles left intact) or a lumpectomy (in which only the tumor and the immediately surrounding tissue are removed) with axillary node dissection (removal of the underarm lymph nodes). If you choose a lumpectomy, you will also need to receive radiation.

It was once believed that removing all the breast tissue (as in the mastectomy) was a safer option, but studies have shown that survival rates following the two types of surgery are equivalent, as long as the lumpectomy is followed by radiation. In patients whose cancer is locally advanced (but has not spread beyond the breasts), the medical oncologist might opt to treat with *chemotherapy* (potent drug therapy) prior to surgery or radiation.

Adjuvant chemotherapy (therapy to destroy remaining, nonvisible cancer cells after surgical treatment) is now the standard of care for premenopausal women with lesions larger than 1 centimeter, and postmenopausal women with estrogen-negative tumors (tumors that are not stimulated by estrogen). Tamoxifen, a drug that opposes estrogen, has proven effective in preventing tumor recurrence. It is even being tested as a preventive agent in women who are at high risk for developing breast cancer.

Women with Stage I disease generally have a 70 to 75 percent chance of surviving ten years. Adjuvant therapy can increase that chance.

Benign Breast Disease

Fortunately, about 80 percent of all breast lumps turn out to be benign. Your gynecologist is usually in a position of central importance to educate, screen, and counsel you about both benign and malignant conditions of the breast. Benign breast diseases include nonmalignant growths like fibroadenomas and lipomas, intraductal papillomas (abnormal proliferations of cells in the milk ducts), and fibrocystic changes (a condition in which the breasts often become lumpier prior to menstruation). Signs of benign breast disease, like signs of breast cancer, include palpable lumps and nipple discharge. Because it is impossible for you to determine whether your symptoms stem from cancer or a benign condition, you should report all unusual breast symptoms to your doctor.

Lipomas. A soft, mobile, fatty tumor, the lipoma is most frequently found in postmenopausal women. Lipomas are relatively common. The treatment: surgical excision.

Fibroadenomas. Fibroadenomas account for 15 to 20 percent of all breast disease. They can occur at any age, including in peri- and postmenopausal women, but are more frequently detected in the twenty- to forty-year-old age group. These lesions feel like discrete, solid masses. They are painless, mobile, and rubbery in consistency. Up to 25 percent of women have multiple fibroadenomas in their breasts, though it is more common to find a single tumor. Fibroadenomas may regress, persist, or enlarge. In women over twenty-five, the usual recommendation is surgical removal.

Intraductal papillomas. Intraductal papillomas are abnormal growths in the milk ducts and are the principal cause of nipple discharge in nonpregnant and nonlactating women. They occur most frequently from ages forty-five to fifty. Intraductal papillomas are the most common cause of bloody nipple discharge; 20 to 50 percent of women with this type of growth experience this symptom. About 90 percent of women with intraductal papillomas also have a palpable mass, which is usually located below or within half an inch of the areola. Between 10 and 15 percent of patients have multiple intraductal papillomas in one or both breasts.

Fibrocystic changes. The term fibrocystic change has been used to describe a spectrum of physiologic changes in the breast. The condition is generally characterized by multiple cysts, or extremely fibrous breast tissue that feels somewhat lumpy. Some women with fibrocystic changes experience breast soreness prior to their menstrual periods. The condition appears to be more common in women who have never had children. Women with an early onset of menses, late menopause, and irregular nonovulatory cycles also appear to have fibrocystic changes more often. Oral contraceptive pills help reduce pain and lumpiness in up to 90 percent of women within three to six months of beginning treatment. Following discontinuation of the pill, however, 30 to 40 percent of women experience recurrent symptoms.

The oral contraceptive pill also appears to reduce the *risk* of benign breast disease, especially in women who have used it for more than five years. (Most notably, it decreases the risk of fibroadenomas and fibrocystic changes.) Risk factors for benign disease include never having children and high intake of caffeine.

Nipple Discharge

Like breast lumps, nipple discharge can be a concern. Though nipple discharge is sometimes associated with breast cancer, it is more often caused by benign breast conditions. Nipple discharge may even be triggered by some medications, including oral contraceptive pills, some tranquilizers, and antidepressants.

A *milky discharge* (galactorrhea) that is bilateral, is spontaneous, and originates from multiple ducts around the nipple can be associated with pregnancy, hypothyroidism, or pituitary tumors (elevated levels of prolactin, the pituitary hormone that stimulates the production of breast milk, tips the doctor off to the existence of such a tumor).

A *pus-filled discharge* is produced by breast infection (mastitis), which requires antibiotic treatment.

When nipple discharge is *clear or watery, yellow, pink or bloody*, a breast biopsy is needed to rule out an underlying cancer. However, two-thirds of women with bloody or clear discharge will actually have the benign condition intraductal papilloma. In cases where there is an underlying carcinoma, 80 percent of patients will have positive cancer cells in the discharge. There is also usually a lump as well, though up to 13 percent of cancers are not palpable. Mammography will detect many of these.

In summary, breast cancer can be cured in the early stages. Remember: mammography, annual examinations, and regular self-examinations are the keys to early diagnosis.

14
Gynecologic Conditions

We discuss in this chapter some of the gynecologic problems that women encounter in the years before and after menopause. We divide our discussion into three parts that correspond to a woman's adult phases: gynecologic conditions most common during the premenopausal or climacteric period; those most common in the decade or so after menopause; and those most prevalent among older women (sixty-five and over). There is some overlap, in that some problems span both the premenopausal and postmenopausal periods, and others continue into old age. But many of the conditions are specific to the particular hormone environment associated with the particular phase of life in which we classify them. Knowledge of these conditions will diminish needless anxiety, and enable you to participate in intelligent decisions about your health care.

The Premenopausal Years

Because the risks of malignancy start to rise at this stage of life, gynecologic symptoms take on a new meaning. It is important that your gynecologist be able to reassure you if you are complaining of excessive menstrual flow or bleeding between menstrual periods. You want to know that these symptoms do not represent any significant disease.

Indeed, irregular bleeding in a forty-four-year-old woman has greater significance than in a twenty-two-year-old—it is more likely to stem from underlying disease, rather than a simple hormonal (also known as functional) disorder. Uterine fibroids (muscle tumors of the uterus) and endometriosis (endometrial tissue that is growing outside of the uterus) become more prevalent in this age group. And if these conditions are ever going to give trouble, it will be during the premenopausal years.

Cervical cancer, too, more commonly strikes in the decade prior to menopause. And a variety of less serious conditions, including premenstrual syndrome (PMS), can give rise to common gynecologic symptoms. (By the same token, it is possible to have disease in the pelvic area that does not produce any symptoms at all. For this reason, regular physical exams are of the utmost importance.) Only your doctor can determine the cause of your symptoms: do not let the fear of serious illness prevent you from seeking medical care.

Abnormal Uterine Bleeding

It is difficult to define an "abnormal" menstrual flow, especially because what may be normal for one patient in terms of frequency and intensity of bleeding may be totally abnormal for another. A periodic hemoglobin count can detect anemia, which would suggest excessive bleeding. But as long as a woman's health seems to be unimpaired, there is usually little reason to regard minor alterations in the menstrual cycle as an abnormality.

As a general rule, frequent and profuse bleeding between menstrual cycles should be investigated. (Patients in whom the menstrual flow is regular but profuse have a condition called *men-*

orrhagia; the term *metrorrhagia* refers to bleeding that occurs at times other than the normal expected date of menstruation.) Abnormal bleeding among women in the thirty-five to forty-five age group can be hormonal in nature, that is, not associated with a diseased organ, though in this age group, conditions like polyps (another type of benign growth) and fibroids can frequently cause this symptom. Uterine cancer is always a possibility, though bleeding is more likely to be associated with uterine cancer in the postmenopausal period. (A diagnosis of hormonal disease is usually one of exclusion. In other words, organic diseases such as fibroids and polyps must first be ruled out.)

Various systemic illnesses, such as thyroid disease, can affect the body by producing abnormal menstrual function. We must also remember that as long as a woman remains in her reproductive years, there is always a chance that abnormal bleeding may be related to ectopic pregnancy, a threatened miscarriage, or other pregnancy-related causes. Physicians are trained to determine the origin of abnormal bleeding.

The gynecologist can use one of two principal tools to manage these problems: an endometrial aspiration or an operation called dilation and curettage (D and C). The D and C, in which the cervix is dilated and tissue is scraped off the uterine lining, is both a diagnostic and therapeutic method. Using this technique, the gynecologist can feel the inside of the uterus and produce tissue for a pathologist to examine. Many physicians are now doing diagnostic D and Cs on an outpatient basis, under local or general anesthesia. In some cases, a D and C also reduces the abnormal bleeding.

Once organic disease is ruled out, hormone therapy can be utilized to regulate the menstrual cycle. Treatment should not be given, however, until a definite diagnosis is made, and serious abnormalities (such as malignancy) are ruled out.

Dysmenorrhea (Cramps)

Dysmenorrhea may or may not be associated with pelvic disease. Some of the causes of painful menses at this stage of life are chronic pelvic infection, relaxation of the ligaments supporting the uterus as a result of childbearing, and endometriosis. The treatment of dysmenorrhea depends on the diagnosis: the physician must rule out the various possibilities mentioned in the preceding paragraphs. (*Secondary dysmenorrhea* refers to painful periods stemming from an underlying disease; *primary dysmenorrhea* is the term used to describe painful menses in which the cause is unknown.)

Pelvic Pain

One of the most common medical complaints among all age groups is lower abdominal pain. Women who experience pain in the lower abdomen tend to automatically attribute the problem to their reproductive organs. At least 50 percent of the time, however, the pain stems from a nongynecologic condition. Sometimes pain can be traced to diseases of the urinary tract, the gastrointestinal system, or the skeletal system. Any one of a variety of abnormalities—alone or in combination—can produce symptoms in this area. For this reason, pelvic pain can be a difficult problem to treat.

The following are some of the nongynecologic causes of pelvic pain:

Urinary tract

- Infections
- Stones of the bladder or urinary tract
- Failure to urinate

Intestinal problems

- Appendicitis
- Constipation
- Diverticulitis (inflammation of a small pouch in the large intestine)
- Irritable bowel syndrome
- Colitis (inflammation of large intestine)
- Cancer of large intestine

Orthopedic problems

- Poor posture
- Stress or injury
- Ruptured disk
- Arthritis
- Scoliosis (spinal curvature)
- Muscle inflammation and irritations

It is impossible to outline in detail all the symptoms that would help a physician to arrive at a differential diagnosis for each of these conditions. But it is important to understand that there are multiple separate and combined nongynecologic causes of pain in the lower abdomen and pelvis.

Of course, the list of gynecologic conditions that cause pelvic pain is also long and varied. Since most of the causes of pain are minor, it is wrong to jump to the premature conclusion that one is dealing with a serious problem such as ovarian cysts or cancer. Infections of the fallopian tubes and ovaries, threatened miscarriage, and ectopic pregnancy can all cause pain.

To pinpoint the source of the pain, the physician will take a careful history, asking questions about the intensity and duration of pain, as well as its relationship to the menstrual cycle.

Sometimes pelvic pain is psychosomatic, in which case it is very difficult to evaluate. The diagnosis of emotional illness usually comes after organic disease is ruled out. Laparoscopy, a procedure in which a scope is inserted through a tiny opening in the abdomen so that the physician can view the patient's pelvic organs, is often the ultimate diagnostic test: it allows for an accurate determination of whether or not an organic disease is present.

The gynecologic causes of pelvic pain include:

Mittelschmerz. Mittelschmerz is characterized by cyclical pain, which usually occurs in one side of the lower abdomen around the time of ovulation (that is, fourteen days before the next period is due). The pain usually lasts from twenty-four to forty-eight hours, and may be accompanied by a small amount of vaginal bleeding. Pain is due to ovulation, which produces a small amount of blood from the ovary that irritates the lining of the abdominal cavity. This irritation shortly subsides, and the pain decreases within eighteen hours. The diagnosis is made by the cyclic nature of the pain and its distinct relationship to the menstrual cycle.

Tubal infection. An acutely inflamed fallopian tube causes severe pelvic pain that is usually one-sided. Acute tubal infections characteristically come on after the menstrual cycle and are often associated with severe pain, a vaginal discharge, and fever. Chronic pelvic infection differs from the acute phase (the onset of the infection). The pain associated with chronic infection is of a deeper, more grinding nature, because of the involvement of nerve roots, and may radiate down the legs.

Ovarian cysts. Ovarian cysts in general are not painful. However, if they twist on their blood supply, they can block blood flow and get acutely inflamed, causing severe one-sided abdominal pain that often radiates down the upper thigh and leg. The pain usually requires immediate consultation with a physician.

Endometriosis. Pain caused by endometriosis is characteristically associated with the menstrual cycle, though the type of pain depends on the site of the endometriosis. If the endometriosis is in the uterine wall, the disease is called *adenomyosis* and generally causes severe menstrual pain. If the endometriosis is located outside the uterus, the pain may only be associated with sexual intercourse. If it involves the intestines or rectum, pain may only be associated with a bowel movement at the time of the menstrual cycle. (See following section for a more in-depth look at endometriosis.)

Pelvic Congestion Syndrome. The term pelvic congestion syndrome (PCS) describes a vague group of symptoms that usually include lower abdominal pain or low backache that is worse during menstruation, fatigue, or emotional upset. Some women also have deep pain on intercourse. The most frequent characteristic of PCS is tenderness of the cervix and uterus on palpation by the gynecologist. Most investigators feel that this syndrome is related to emotional factors. What is seen on examination of women with PCS is a congestion of the veins in the pelvic organs. Even though the organic changes do occur, most physicians feel that the origin of PCS is psychosomatic. There is some controversy as to whether or not the syndrome actually exists. The treatment is oriented along these lines. (PCS often goes along with PMS.)

Pelvic pain is common enough that most women will experience various types of discomfort throughout their menstruating years. Most of the causes are hormonal, and are not of much concern. Your gynecologist is your best guide to what is significant and what is functional. However, your understanding of the anatomy, physiology, and causes of the pain will go a long way toward helping allay anxiety, and will also enable you to participate in your care.

Premenstrual Syndrome (PMS)

Many women experience a wide spectrum of symptoms in the days immediately preceding the onset of their menstrual periods. These symptoms—which may include emotional instability, irritability, lack of concentration, insomnia, headache, painful breasts, abdominal distention, bearing-down pelvic discomfort, urinary frequency, constipation, and loss of appetite—are together referred to as premenstrual tension, or premenstrual syndrome. In some women, PMS-like symptoms stem from organic disease, such as endometriosis, but in many women, there is no evidence of pelvic abnormalities. In fact, except for the ten days or so prior to menstruation, these women are usually symptom-free.

How a woman responds to premenstrual changes depends in part on her emotional state. But it is clear that these symptoms do occur. Sometimes they give rise to fears of emotional illness, adding to depression and a general sense of ill health. PMS also appears to affect behavior: statistics indicate that 80 percent of the major crimes committed by women occur during the premenstrual phase of their cycle. It is probable that most women experience some discomfort during this phase, and perhaps 50 percent of women at some point have symptoms so severe that they interfere with day-to-day life and require treatment.

Some experts think that PMS is due to increased fluid retention that results from premenstrual hormonal activity. (Symptoms of irritability, headaches, and emotional instability may even be due to fluid retention in the brain.) The treatment of PMS, therefore, is based on the concept that there is an excess of salt and water in the body. The following treatments are recommended:

1. Restriction of fluids, especially coffee and other caffeine-containing beverages
2. The use of diuretic drugs to promote fluid elimination
3. The use of various types of tranquilizing drugs
4. Education as to the cause of the syndrome and reassurance by the physician
5. Exercise

Endometriosis

Endometriosis is one of the most unusual diseases in the field of gynecology. It is caused by the presence of implants of endometrial tissue (the cells that line the uterus) in areas other than the endometrial cavity of the uterus. These implants respond to the menstrual hormones, despite the fact that they are no longer situated in the endometrial cavity. The disease, therefore, is symptomatic only during the years of menstrual activity, and the symptoms tend to be cyclic, like the menstrual cycle.

The cause of endometriosis is still unknown, although there are two general theories. One theory (known as *retrograde menstruation*) suggests that in some women, menstrual matter is extruded from the uterus through both the vagina and the fallopian tubes. This endometrial tissue is then free to implant in the pelvic cavity, where it responds to cyclic hormonal stimulation. The other hypothesis suggests that endometriosis arises from embryonic implants that exist at birth, which slowly react to cyclic hormonal stimulation and grow. Endometriosis is not, however, considered to be hereditary.

There are two types of endometriosis: *adenomyosis*, where endometrial tissue furrows into the uterine wall itself, forming lesions; and *pelvic endometriosis*, where endometrial lesions are found on the surface of the uterus, ovaries, bowel, or abdominal cavity lining.

There are also two types of symptoms associated with endometriosis. One is lower abdominal pain, which comes on just before the menstrual cycle. This pain consists of a vague bearing-down discomfort that sometimes radiates into the thighs. The second symptom is dysmenorrhea, or pain during menses, that becomes progressively worse over time. The intensity of the pain varies from woman to woman; in fact, 25 percent of patients who are diagnosed with endometriosis experience no pain at all. Other symptoms that may be associated with the condition are lower back pain and painful deep intercourse at the time of the menstrual cycle. In advanced endometriosis involving the large bowel, blood may be found in the stool during menses, due to bleeding from endometrial implants on the bowel wall. In general, symptoms tend to progress as endometriosis spreads and grows. However, the process goes away after menopause.

The diagnosis of endometriosis is made by specific findings on pelvic examination, such as nodular growths behind the uterus that are quite tender. Laparoscopic viewing of the pelvic organs will also provide a definitive diagnosis.

The treatment of the disease depends upon a woman's age, her symptoms, and her desire for procreation, since endometriosis can cause infertility by producing scarring on the fallopian tubes and ovaries. Because it is a benign disease that occurs only during the menstruating years, most doctors treat endometriosis conservatively. Once ovarian function ceases, the disease rapidly diminishes.

Generally, treatment is indicated when a patient experiences severe pain or infertility. There are three basic treatment plans:

1. Observation, with symptomatic treatment (e.g., painkillers to alleviate pain)
2. Medical treatment with hormonal drugs
3. Surgical removal of the endometriosis or the diseased organs

Drugs like estrogen and progesterone—or birth control pills—are designed to inhibit ovulation. The rationale for the use of these drugs is that endometriosis regresses during pregnancy, probably because ovulation is suppressed. Therefore, the aim of medical therapy is to inhibit ovulation for approximately nine months, during which time much of the endometriosis will dry up.

Depending on the severity of the disease, surgery may be indicated. The most conservative surgery, which can often be done through a laparoscope, is removal of the endometriosis itself, wherever possible. The nerves leading to the pelvic area may also be cut, diminishing any pain associated with the disease. This operation is called a *presacral neurectomy*. A more aggressive approach, which is reserved for women with extensive symptoms who no longer want to preserve childbearing capacity, is hysterectomy, or removal of the entire uterus. Some physicians believe the ovaries can be preserved in hysterectomy cases, but this point is controversial.

Fibroids of the Uterus

The most common type of uterine growth in the premenopausal woman is a benign tumor known as a uterine fibroid. Approximately one out of five women over the age of thirty has fibroids, though they vary widely in size, shape, and location within the uterus. These fibroids are estrogen-sensitive; as with endometriosis, their growth within the uterine muscle depends on cyclic ovarian function. In other words, they regress after menopause.

The fibroid thus makes its appearance in reproductive-aged women, with the highest incidence noted in the latter half of the menstrual years. African-American women are particularly susceptible to fibroids, probably due to as-yet-unknown genetic factors.

There are basically three types of fibroid growths based on their site, which determines symptoms, and, therefore, the need for treatment. Remember that the vast majority of fibroids are benign.

Intramural fibroids develop within the uterine walls. They are the most common. They can get very large, but they rarely produce symptoms unless they reach the size of a three- to four-month pregnancy.

Subserosal fibroids grow on the outer surface of the uterus. They, too, must become quite large before producing symptoms.

Submucous fibroids occur within the endometrium, or lining, of the uterus. Because of their location, they can interfere with menstrual function and cause menorrhagia, or excessive menstrual flow, thereby producing secondary anemia, weakness, and dizziness. If submucous fibroids do produce menorrhagia, treatment is required.

Diagnosis of a fibroid is made by physical examination: the uterus is usually enlarged. Pinpointing the location of a fibroid is usually done with a D and C, with or without hysteroscopy (a procedure in which a scope is inserted through the cervix to enable the doctor to view the uterus); with an X-ray technique called a hysterogram; or with sonography.

Subserosal or intramural fibroids rarely require surgery unless they are very large, press upon the bladder and cause frequent urination, or undergo degeneration, producing pain or pressure on the bowel. These symptoms are relatively rare. Despite their ability to grow quite large, fibroids rarely cause pain. In fact, sometimes they don't require any treatment at all. If a submucous fibroid causes bleeding, surgery may be required to prevent or treat anemia.

The decision for or against therapy depends on a patient's symptoms, the growth pattern and location of the fibroid, the age and general health of the patient, and her wishes regarding having children. The three main forms of treatment include conservative observation; surgery of a conservative nature, wherein the fibroids themselves are removed, leaving the uterus (this operation is called a *myomectomy*, or, if done through the hysteroscope, a *hysteroscopic resection*); or a hysterectomy, in which the fibroids and the uterus are removed with or without preservation of the ovaries.

If surgery is indicated because of symptoms, conservative surgery such as myomectomy or hysteroscopic resection should be considered. A woman can still establish and maintain a pregnancy even after multiple myomectomies, despite the extensive nature of the process. But all too often, operations are suggested to women for fibroids that are asymptomatic. This type of treatment should be avoided. Remember, fibroids regress after menopause.

A word regarding second opinions about gynecologic surgery: gynecologists' opinions will often differ as to the indications for gynecologic surgery, even if they are equally reassuring and well meaning. It is always in your best interest to get a second opinion before undergoing any gynecologic operation. Many medical insurance companies recognize this, and will often pay for the consultation. If the two surgeons disagree, get a third opinion.

Ovarian Growths

The ovary is one of the most active organs in the body during the menstruating years, undergoing changes on a monthly basis. Ovulation requires the development each cycle of small fluid-filled sacs, or *follicles*, that encase the eggs. Unfortunately, sometimes these sacs do not disappear when they should. They grow and give rise to so-called benign ovarian cysts—the most common form of ovarian growth. The majority of cysts do not produce symptoms, though sometimes cysts may cause irregularity in the menstrual cycle. They generally disappear with time, and usually the only treatment required is observation.

Occasionally, however, cysts can twist or outgrow their blood supply and cause pain, in which case the cyst—or possibly even an ovary—might have to be surgically removed. But first a definitive diagnosis must be made. Cysts are diagnosed on pelvic examination, but it is not always possible to distinguish between a benign and malignant growth without a biopsy. In addition, there are many types of ovarian growths—both benign and malignant. The final diagnosis rests on a pathologist's interpretation of tissue obtained by the surgeon.

Gynecologic Cancer

Cancer of a woman's reproductive organs has a potentially tremendous emotional impact. It can affect the most sensitive, personal aspects of her life. Depending on the type of cancer, the patient is faced with the personal trauma of changes in lifestyle, removal of reproductive capacity, and anatomical changes in sex organs. This is compounded by the normal fears associated with cancer—fear of illness, pain, dependency, and possible death. Worries about the financial burdens associated with major long-term illness are also overwhelming.

Unfortunately, almost every woman in her lifetime is in one way or another affected by cancer, whether it strikes a family member, close friend, or herself. However, misinformation regarding cancer is prevalent in our society. Despite the many changes and advances in the treatment of the disease, people still continue to imagine that the disease is uniformly incurable. This belief can paralyze people, preventing them from seeking medical attention in the early stages when the disease is curable. It is crucial to understand that most of the common cancers in women are highly curable if caught in the early stages. Although parts of this section may be frightening, knowledge is one of the most important weapons in fighting cancer.

What is unique about most of the reproductive organs (except the ovaries) is that they are readily accessible for early diagnosis—and therefore treatment. Because of this, most gynecologic cancers have a high cure rate. However, with the exception of breast cancer, which can be found on self-examination, early detection is impossible without physical examination by a physician.

Because cancer is the second leading cause of death in women (see list on page 186), it is advisable to get periodic examinations from an early age. And because the incidence of malignancies in women increases with age, regular checkups become even more important as you approach menopause.

Fortunately, because women today are better informed about their health, they seek early care and diagnosis, and cancer treatment is started sooner. In fact, despite the increasing incidence of malignancy, cure rates are higher than ever—and the life expectancy of women diagnosed with cancer has increased. This is due in part to an increase in diagnostic accuracy and improved treatment facilities, but it is also related to early detection. With any cancer, time is of the essence. Therefore, any delay in seeking medical care may significantly affect the ultimate outcome.

Ten Leading Causes of Death in Women of All Ages

1. Heart Disease
2. Cancer
3. Cerebrovascular accident (blood clots or hemorrhage in the brain)
4. Accidents
5. Pneumonia and influenza
6. Diabetes
7. Suicide
8. Cirrhosis of the liver (scarring and destruction of liver often due to excessive alcohol use)
9. Kidney diseases
10. Arteriosclerosis (hardening of the arteries)

Source: Centers for Disease Control, 1988

Again, the importance of yearly checkups and physical examinations—including breast examinations and Pap smears from an early age on—cannot be stressed enough. Early diagnosis is the key to curability and success.

Cancer is characterized by the unrestricted growth of cells within an organ, resulting in the breakdown of tissue and the invasion and eventual destruction of the surrounding normal tissue. Cancer cells also break off from their local sites, and can be carried by the blood and lymph channels to other parts of the body, where they continue to grow and destroy other organs and tissues. These cells are not governed by the disciplined behavior of normal cells: they basically wreak havoc wherever they go.

Cancer is most apt to occur in the lungs, breast, intestines,

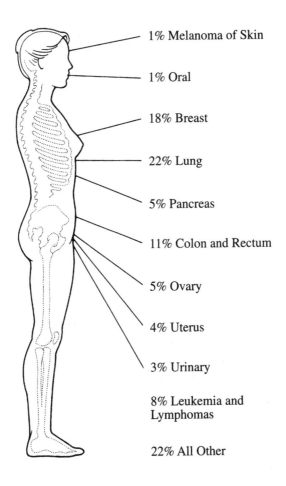

1% Melanoma of Skin

1% Oral

18% Breast

22% Lung

5% Pancreas

11% Colon and Rectum

5% Ovary

4% Uterus

3% Urinary

8% Leukemia and Lymphomas

22% All Other

FIGURE 11 *1993 estimated percentage of women's deaths from cancer by cancer type.*

and uterus. There are many different types of malignancies, the names of which are derived from the types of tissue from which the malignancy originates. A malignancy that arises in glandular tissue (such as the breast or uterus) is called an *adenocarcinoma*. A malignancy that originates in epithelial tissue (such as the lining of the vagina or cervix) is called *squamous cell carcinoma*. The degree of malignancy varies widely, so generalizations regarding treatment and cure are difficult.

Symptoms also vary. For instance, cancer of the ovaries is relatively asymptomatic until the late stages of the disease. The ovaries are also relatively inaccessible for examination. Therefore, diagnosis is more difficult, and cure rates are lower. Uterine cancer, on the other hand, tends to produce abnormal bleeding, making it easier to identify. Cancer of the cervix can easily be diagnosed by a Pap smear in the very early stages, and thus is now virtually 100 percent curable—assuming regular Pap tests.

The transformation of cells from normal to malignant can be a gradual process, occurring over a period of years. Scientists believe there are various trigger mechanisms that account for the changes. Smoking, for example, is a trigger mechanism for lung cancer and cervical cancer. Similarly, postmenopausal estrogen could be considered a trigger mechanism for cancer of the uterus. An understanding of what trigger mechanisms do, of course, is very important in cancer prevention.

The factors that determine the ability of a tumor to advance are still unknown, though genetic, immunologic, and nutritional factors have all been considered. Much of cancer research today is focused on understanding what controls cancer at the cellular level. Furthering our understanding of the disease process may help us devise strategies to enhance our defenses against cancer.

Cancer is not a single disease. It is a vast group of diseases varying in type, site, degree of differentiation, and prognosis.

Each type of malignancy will be discussed in the section on the life phase in which it is most common. Cervical cancer, especially in its early stages, is most common between the ages of forty and fifty, so it is discussed in this section. Ovarian and uterine cancer, most prevalent among women ages fifty to sixty-five, will be discussed in the section on peri- and postmenopausal women (see pages 197 and 198); cancer of the vulva and vagina are more common in old age and will be discussed in the section on older age (see page 206).

Cancer of the Cervix

The early, noninvasive forms of cervical cancer, cervical dysplasia, and cancer in situ are most common between thirty and forty years of age. The advanced, invasive form of the disease usually strikes women in their forties. Invasive cancer generally does not occur until approximately ten years after the appearance of in situ disease. The term *in situ* is used to describe cell changes that meet all the criteria for malignancy, except that the element of invasion is absent. In other words, the malignancy is confined to the surface of the tissue. The time element required for progression of in situ cancer to invasive cancer is the key to our ability to obtain high cure rates—if the cancer is diagnosed early.

Once invasion of the underlying tissue occurs, bleeding from the cervix is common. Invasive cervical cancer is associated with bleeding following intercourse and staining between periods; a watery discharge may also be present. Early cervical cancer, however, is asymptomatic—and rarely shows up on a physical exam. Your doctor is usually alerted to the presence of cervical cancer by an abnormal Pap smear, though examination of cervical tissue by biopsy is required before a definitive diagnosis can be made.

The cause of cervical cancer is unknown. However, studies have shown a correlation between early sexual intercourse (and early childbirth) and this cancer. Its incidence appears to be markedly lower among virgins. It is most likely that intercourse is the principal factor involved, rather than childbearing. Early intercourse with multiple sexual partners is also a significant factor in the development of the disease. Some experts believe that certain sexually transmitted diseases, like the herpes virus and the human papilloma virus, may be linked to the eventual development of cervical cancer.

Women who are married to circumcised men also have a significantly lower incidence of the disease, probably because the foreskin provides a sanctuary in which infectious agents like viruses can proliferate. Other factors that have been implicated in the development of cervical cancer are cigarette smoking and nutritional deficiencies.

Since carcinoma in situ is confined to a small area and is slow to develop, it lends itself to cure. The relatively slow growth pattern of cervical cancer is taken into consideration in the treatment of the disease. Whereas hysterectomy may be a satisfactory cure for a woman who has completed her family, it may not be a happy—or indicated—one for the patient who is contemplating a family or wants to have more children. Carcinoma in situ can be treated by local excision, particularly in the woman who wants to preserve her reproductive organs.

Like breast cancer, cervical cancer is classified in stages:

Stage 0. Carcinoma in situ.

Stage I. Disease confined to cervix, but invasive.

Stage II. Malignancy extends beyond cervix but does not reach lateral pelvic walls, although it may involve upper part of vagina.

Stage III. Disease has spread to pelvic wall or lower third of vagina.

Stage IV. Cancer involves bladder and rectum, or other distant spread.

There is a direct relationship between the stage of the malignancy and the eventual cure rate.

In situ cancer (Stage 0) is generally treated in one of three ways. In the young woman who still wants to have children, the cervix can be simply treated by freezing (*cryosurgery*), heating (*cauterization*), or surgical excision of the cancer (called *conization*, because the surgeon removes a cone-shaped piece of the cervix). It is important after these therapies to have Pap smears done at least two to three times during the first year of follow-up.

If the patient with Stage 0 cancer has completed her family and has no desire to have children, has no strong emotional reasons for preserving childbearing capacity, and has no strong emotional reasons for preserving menstrual function, a hysterectomy can be done. There is no reason, however, to remove the ovaries.

If a patient is pregnant when the Stage 0 lesion is diagnosed, the pregnancy may be allowed to continue. The doctor can view the cervix with a *colposcope* (a scope that is inserted through the vagina) to follow the abnormal changes. A cone biopsy, however, should be carried out during pregnancy if there is a suspicion of invasive cancer.

Stage I cancer of the cervix is most commonly treated by an operation called a *radical hysterectomy*. A radical hysterectomy involves the removal of the uterus, the ovaries, and the surrounding pelvic tissue, including the lymph nodes. Some doctors favor *radium* (a radioactive substance that is introduced in the cervical region for localized radiation treatment) and other forms of radiation therapy for the treatment of Stage I cancer. The five-year survival rate (patients alive five years after diagnosis) for Stage I disease is up to 90 percent.

Stage II cervical cancer may also be treated with radical surgery, but is usually treated with radiation. However, the five-year survival rate is only around 60 percent.

Stages III and IV are treated by a combination of chemotherapy and radiation. The five-year cure rates for stage III and IV are only 27 percent and 7 percent, respectively. Despite these gloomy statistics, remember that the vast majority of cervical cancers are stage 0 and stage I, both of which are highly curable. The key is early diagnosis by routine Pap smears.

The Menopausal and Postmenopausal Years

Many physicians advise twice-a-year examinations during the perimenopausal period, both from a physiological point of view and for educational support. Because of the many changes taking place, some women will benefit from continued dialogue with their physician. Symptoms that should be reported to your physician include:

- Prolongation of menstrual flow beyond seven days
- Intermenstrual spotting or bleeding
- Bleeding following intercourse or douching
- Increased amount of blood flow with gushing or clots
- Increase in size of abdomen
- Persistent pelvic pressure or low back pain
- Pain with intercourse

Abnormal Bleeding

Abnormal uterine bleeding due to hormonal changes is common in this phase, especially in the years preceding the cessation of menstrual flow. The irregular bleeding that occurs prior to menopause is similar in nature to that which occurs during puberty and adolescence. In youth, however, the abnormal bleeding stemmed from immaturity of the ovaries; in the perimenopausal years, this symptom is caused by aging ovaries that cease to respond in the usual way to pituitary stimulation.

As your estrogen levels fall, and your cycles become increasingly anovulatory, bleeding patterns may change. You can expect an occasional period that is longer and heavier—more than the usual amount of blood. However, if this pattern establishes itself and the flow is excessive, medical help is indicated.

Your physician will evaluate your present menstrual pattern with regard to your previous menstrual pattern. At this time of life, the periods may be very short, very long, too frequent, or too delayed in interval. Most gynecologists feel, though, that the safest approach is to rule out underlying disease—especially submucous fibroids or malignancy. As in the case of premenopausal bleeding, your doctor will probably perform an endometrial aspiration or a D and C to diagnose the problem. (A D and C may actually help regulate the bleeding if the bleeding stems from hormonal changes.)

Other findings on D and C might include *adenomatous hyperplasia* (an overgrowth of the uterine lining) or endometrial polyps. Adenomatous hyperplasia is one of the causes of excessive menstrual flow in the perimenopausal years. A premalignant lesion in the endometrium, it is analogous to in situ cancer of the cervix. If a D and C should reveal adenomatous hyperplasia, a hysterectomy may be indicated. Hormonal therapy may be another alternative.

Endometrial polyps are also a frequent finding on D and C at this time of life, and may provide another explanation for excessive uterine bleeding. Polyps are small growths on the endometrium that are easily removed during the D and C. They are most often benign; their removal will prevent further symptomatology.

Because uterine fibroids may continue to grow until the cessation of menstrual function, they continue to cause problems during the perimenopausal period. But conservative management of the problem is especially called for at this stage. If a fibroid is just beginning to cause abnormal menstrual function at age forty-nine, it may only require another year of watchful waiting (prior to the cessation of menstrual flow) to get by without a hysterectomy.

Problems in the Pelvic Supporting Structures

Over the course of a woman's life, problems and weaknesses can arise in her vagina, vulva, and the ligaments supporting her bladder, rectum, and uterus. These structures may have been damaged or weakened during a difficult delivery, or as a result of multiple pregnancies. Occasionally these problems arise because of genetic predisposition.

As aging occurs, the ligaments supporting the pelvic organs and the muscles in this area can become weaker and eventually lead to three well-recognized types of pelvic defects. They involve prolapses, or "dropping," of the various organs. The prolapses vary in degree depending on the amount of damage to the structures, and for the most part occur in combination, although on rare occasions they are present as single events. The three types of prolapses are called *cystocele*, the dropping of the bladder into the vagina (a *urethrocele* is a prolapse of the urethra into the vagina); *rectocele*, a protrusion of the rectum into the vagina; and *uterine prolapse,* a prolapse of the entire uterus, due to weakness of the supports of the uterus itself.

Cystocele and urethrocele. A defect in the bladder and urethral supports within the upper walls of the vagina results in extrusion of these organs into the vagina. Resulting symptoms may include a bearing-down discomfort in the vagina and *stress incontinence,* a loss of urine when coughing, laughing, or sneezing. Recurrent urinary tract infection (such as cystitis) is also commonly associated with a cystocele. A physician can diagnose these conditions by pelvic examination. Surgery is usually the treatment of choice when indicated. The indications for surgery are severe stress incontinence, an enlarging protrusion, or recurrent bouts of cystitis. Surgery consists of a vaginal operation in which the defects are corrected by strengthening the muscles and ligaments that support these organs.

Rectocele. The rectocele is a herniation of the rectum toward the vagina due to weakness of the supporting muscles and ligaments. The defect usually originates after a difficult vaginal delivery and develops slowly over the years. A rectocele rarely causes symptoms. Occasionally, a bearing-down feeling is present, and when a rectocele becomes large, it may be difficult to fully empty the rectum on defecation. A physician can diagnose a rectocele by pelvic examination. Treatment is also surgical: a vaginal reconstruction operation is necessary to repair the damaged tissues.

Uterine prolapse. Previous obstetrical trauma is also the main cause of a dropping or weakening of the uterus. Uterine prolapse is categorized by degree: when the uterus has descended into the vaginal canal but has not yet descended to the vaginal opening, it is referred to as *first-degree prolapse.* In *second-degree pro-*

lapse, the cervix appears—partially or completely—outside the vaginal orifice. In *third-degree, or complete, prolapse,* the complete descent of the uterus results in the entire organ hanging out of the vagina.

Except for occasional bearing-down discomfort, first-degree prolapse is generally not associated with symptoms. With second- and third-degree prolapse, however, women become increasingly aware of this bearing-down discomfort, and the size of the protruding mass increases. There may be a general feeling of lack of pelvic support and a sense that the womb is dropping out. With complete prolapse, there is difficulty in sitting and walking. The usual treatment for these symptomatic prolapses is surgical, and the operation of choice depends on the patient's age and medical condition, as well as the type of symptoms and prolapse. Surgery can correct the problem either by removing the uterus (via a vaginal hysterectomy) or by repairing the muscles and ligaments involved and leaving the uterus intact.

Women who have severe medical problems that do not allow surgery can use a supporting plastic or rubber device called a *pessary,* which looks like a large diaphragm and is placed within the vagina to support the uterus in its normal position. However, the pessary must be removed, cleaned, and replaced at monthly intervals. This sort of device is a nuisance, but it is preferable to risking surgery if you are ill.

Occasionally, a woman who is still of childbearing age has prolapse symptoms that require surgery. If at all possible, surgery should be delayed until the woman has finished having children. However, if symptoms of a cystocele, urethrocele, or rectocele warrant treatment, it may be necessary to deliver any subsequent pregnancies by cesarean section to prevent recurrence of the prolapse.

Due to improvements in obstetrical care and the decreasing frequency of difficult forceps deliveries, uterine, vaginal, and rectal prolapses have diminished in the past few years. In addition, surgery to repair them is generally successful. There is certainly no reason for a woman with symptomatic prolapses to avoid surgical treatment and suffer.

Cancer of the Uterus

Cancer of the endometrial lining of the uterus is the most common reproductive cancer. It most often occurs near the menopause, the average age being fifty-five years. Doctors do not know the cause of endometrial cancer, but we suspect that women who get it have a hormonal predisposition, a genetic predisposition, or both to the disease. As we have discussed, postmenopausal unopposed estrogen replacement therapy has been associated with increased rates of uterine cancer, though the exact role of estrogen in triggering the disease is not known either. Women with diabetes, hypertension, or obesity are also more prone to this disease.

Classic symptoms of uterine cancer are abnormal bleeding, a watery discharge, or both in a postmenopausal woman—any woman with postmenopausal bleeding should have a diagnostic study by aspiration or D and C to rule out the presence of malignancy.

Once endometrial cancer has been diagnosed, treatment depends on the stage of the disease. Treatment usually consists of surgery. Radiation therapy may be required following surgery. The hormone progesterone has been used successfully after surgery in the treatment of this disease in advanced cases. As with most cancers, the earlier the diagnosis is made, the higher the cure rate. Overall, 75 percent of the women with endometrial cancer will be cured.

Cancer of the Ovary

Ovarian cancer is less common than uterine cancer, but the results of treatment are usually poor because of the difficulty in diagnosis. Most ovarian tumors are asymptomatic in the early stages; the only method of diagnosis is pelvic examination, sonography, or a blood test. Once ovarian cancer progresses to the state where it does produce symptoms (Stages III and IV), the cancer is usually not curable, though it can still be treated. We cannot overemphasize the importance of an annual pelvic examination in finding early ovarian growths.

The average age of women who get ovarian cancer is fifty years. There are many different types of ovarian cancer with varying long-term outcomes. The primary method of treatment is surgery in combination with chemotherapy. The results of treatment depend on many variables, including stage, age of the patient, and surgical procedure used. The key to cure, however, is early diagnosis.

Women with a family history of breast cancer, colon cancer, ovarian cancer, or uterine cancer need to be carefully screened for ovarian cancer. Screening the entire population has not been shown to be cost-effective, or to change the survival rate. However, in women with a family history as noted, twice-yearly pelvic examinations, blood tests (known as CA125), and pelvic sonograms should be done.

If your doctor finds a mass and raises the possibility of ovarian cancer, you should request that a gynecologic oncologist be available in the surgical operating room. A gynecologic oncologist is trained in cancer surgery and management of patients with cancer of the reproductive tract.

Hysterectomy

Hysterectomies are usually performed to treat certain gynecologic diseases in women past childbearing age, though occasionally a woman in her twenties or thirties requires removal of her uterus for medical reasons. A hysterectomy is particularly traumatic for a woman who has not yet completed her family, but this type of surgery is emotionally difficult for a woman of any age and regardless of parental status. If you have to have a hysterectomy, a thorough understanding of the procedure may allay some of your apprehension and make the operation easier to accept.

We should begin by pointing out that contrary to popular belief, a hysterectomy does not necessarily mean the removal of all internal reproductive organs—the uterus, the fallopian tubes, and the ovaries. The term *hysterectomy* refers specifically to removal of the uterus (see figure 12), though in some cases an *oophorectomy* (surgical removal of the ovaries), a *bilateral salpingectomy* (removal of the fallopian tubes), or both *(salpingo-oophorectomy)* is indicated as well.

There are four methods of performing a hysterectomy: abdominal, vaginal, cesarean, and laparoscopic-assisted. The abdominal approach, in which the uterus is removed through an abdominal incision, is used in most cases.

Vaginal hysterectomy does not leave an external scar, and though not always practical, it gives superior results in certain situations. It is often the preferred method for women who are extremely overweight, since an internal incision will heal more readily than an abdominal one. Laparoscopy (a method of operating through a small incision in the abdominal wall) can also facilitate doing a hysterectomy through the vagina. Recently we have performed laparoscopic-assisted vaginal hysterectomies allowing the patient to go home in two days.

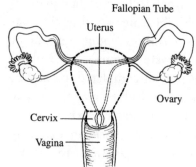

SUBTOTAL HYSTERECTOMY
(body of uterus removed,
cervix remains)

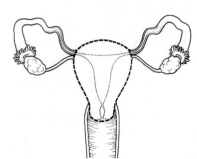

TOTAL HYSTERECTOMY
(entire uterus removed)

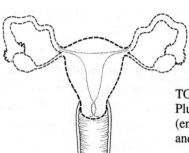

TOTAL HYSTERECTOMY
Plus Bilateral Salpingo-oophorectomy
(entire uterus, fallopian tubes,
and ovaries removed)

FIGURE 12 *Types of hysterectomy.*

A cesarean hysterectomy is performed immediately following a cesarean section, either when hysterectomy has been prearranged as a means of sterilization, or when emergency complications, such as uncontrollable hemorrhage or uterine rupture, require removal of the uterus.

Hysterectomy is a major surgical procedure. The operation itself takes from one to two and a half hours to perform, and requires a four- to five-week hospital stay. Full recovery takes about four to six weeks, during which time intense physical exertion and sexual intercourse must be avoided. The physician will tell the patient when it is safe to resume normal activities.

Many of the gynecologic conditions we have discussed in this chapter may prompt a gynecologist to recommend a hysterectomy, though in most cases, hysterectomy is a treatment of last resort. The following are some of the usual indications for the operation:

Uterine fibroids. Uterine fibroids are the most common reason for hysterectomy. In a young patient, the physician will try to save the uterus and remove only the fibroids (*myomectomy*). A woman who has undergone this operation may still have children by cesarean section. In the older woman—or in the young woman who has completed her family or does not wish to have children— a hysterectomy is the normal procedure. Removal of the uterus eliminates the possibility of developing more fibroids, and also prevents future uterine malignancy. Whether a hysterectomy is required for the removal of fibroids depends on the patient's symptoms, the size of the fibroids, and whether they interfere with physical examination of the ovaries.

Cancer of the cervix. Invasive cervical cancer, the disease that could be virtually eliminated if all women had annual Pap smears, often necessitates a hysterectomy.

Placenta abruptio. In this complication of pregnancy, also known as placenta abruption (or abruptio placenta), the placenta breaks away from the wall of the uterus. The majority of cases can be treated by prompt vaginal delivery or by emergency cesarean section. In rare cases, however, severe hemorrhaging or extreme damage to the uterine wall may make removal of the uterus necessary.

Placenta accreta. Placenta accreta is a complication of pregnancy in which the placenta attaches itself so closely to the wall of the uterus that it cannot be dislodged without destroying the uterine wall. Severe postpartum hemorrhage may result. If it cannot be controlled by such measures as uterine massage, medication, D and C, and other surgical techniques, a hysterectomy may be required.

Dysfunctional uterine bleeding. Irregular and heavy bleeding from the uterus in the absence of organic disease may be another reason for hysterectomy. However, conservative measures such as medication and repeated D and C and endometrial *ablation* (the burning off of the uterine lining by laser or cauterization) are effective in about 80 percent of such cases. Hysterectomy is often considered only as a last resort.

The following conditions may require removal of the ovaries, the fallopian tubes, or both, in addition to removal of the uterus:

Endometriosis. Because this condition can affect all of the reproductive organs (fragments of the uterine lining can attach to the outside of the uterus, as well as to the tubes and ovaries), severe, symptomatic endometriosis may require removal of the uterus together with the tubes and ovaries.

Chronic pelvic infection. The removal of all the reproductive organs may also be indicated for severe pelvic infection.

Other gynecologic cancers. Cancers of the uterine fundus (the body or upper portion of the womb), the endometrium, the ovaries, and the fallopian tubes usually require hysterectomy and removal of the tubes and ovaries.

Some women who need to undergo a hysterectomy fear that they will lose their femininity along with their uterus. We try to explain to our patients, and to their husbands when appropriate, that the uterus has nothing to do with ovarian function, nothing to do with libido, and nothing to do with the enjoyment of intercourse or the occurrence of orgasm. The only changes a woman will experience after having a hysterectomy are losing fertility and no longer menstruating. Unfortunately, cyclical sensations such as bloating or irritability will remain if the ovaries are left in place.

If you are considering this operation, ask your physician for a careful explanation before surgery, so that you can understand the necessity for the operation, begin to anticipate the long-term benefits, and adjust to the situation. You and your physician should participate in this decision.

Older Age (Sixty-five and Over)

One of the questions that occasionally confront an older woman is whether or not to take the risk of elective surgery that will make her more comfortable—and happier—as long as her life continues. Age, itself, is not a contraindication to surgery. Surgery for such conditions as prolapse of the female organs must be evaluated on an individual basis, weighing the medical risks of the surgical procedure against the benefit the surgery will provide.

Questions to Ask Your Doctor
Before a Hysterectomy

- Why do I need to have a hysterectomy?
- What organ or organs will be removed and why?
- Will my ovaries be left in place? If not, why not?
- Will my cervix be removed? If so, why?
- Are there alternatives for me besides a hysterectomy?
- What are the advantages, risks, benefits of each alternative?
- What will be the physical effects of a hysterectomy?
- Are these effects permanent?
- What will happen to my figure, my weight, my breasts?
- How will it affect my sex life?
- Will I experience menopause? Can the symptoms of menopause be treated? What are the risks and benefits of such treatment?
- Will the operation be a vaginal or abdominal hysterectomy? And why?
- What can I expect in the hospital? What pre-operative procedures? What length of stay? What anesthesia? Infection? A transfusion? A urinary catheter?
- What kind of care will I need after my hysterectomy?
- How should I prepare for coming home from the hospital?
- How soon can I go back to work? Try heavy housework?
- When can I resume sexual activity?

Some common gynecological problems at this age are as follows:

Vaginal bleeding. Postmenopausal bleeding from the vagina at this age is very often a serious indicator of potential uterine, vaginal, or cervical cancer, and should not be overlooked. Diagnostic tests should be performed as outlined in the previous sections.

Urologic problems. Changes in the function of the bladder and urinary tract are also more common at this stage, due to hormonal deficiencies. They result in complaints of urinary frequency and urgency.

Prolapse. Prolapse of the female organs, as discussed earlier in this chapter, is even more significant a problem in the older age group, because pelvic muscles and the supporting tissues become increasingly weak with age.

Vaginal infection. Infections of the vaginal tract of a nonserious, annoying nature are commonly due to thinning of the vaginal skin, which decreases resistance to infection. Discharge might be a sign of infection that requires local antibiotic therapy.

Problems Associated with Vulvar Disease

As the effect of hormone withdrawal becomes evident, the vulva become thinner and more atrophic. The pubic hair becomes less abundant, and there is a loss of fat in this area. These changes in the vulva and vagina allow irritation and infection to occur more easily. These infections are troublesome because they produce intense itching and burning. Treatment is directed not only at eliminating the underlying cause of irritation, but also at preventing scratching, which only intensifies the irritation.

Some of the itching that elderly women experience in this area comes from emotional causes, such as stress or sexual frustration, and leads to scratching and irritation. Understanding this might help alleviate the symptom. Local solutions such as cornstarch baths and potassium permanganate, as well as salt-water compresses, help reduce itching and burning. Complete drying of the area after baths is important; a heat lamp or hair dry-er may facilitate drying. Irritation should be avoided. Cotton un-derpants are better than nylon or silk. Certain preparations such as steroids, antihistamines, and local anesthetics may also be of value. However, secondary irritation due to medications is very common, so the physician will watch for this. Any underlying infections such as trichomonas, monilia, or bacterial infections should be treated by the physician.

Problems of the Urinary Tract

Many elderly women complain of frequency, urgency, and burn-ing on urination. Often these symptoms arise without any evi-dence of urinary tract infection. The defect seems to stem from an estrogen deficiency, which produces an irritative, noninfec-tious inflammation of the urinary tract. Once infection has been ruled out and the diagnosis is made, treatment can be institut-ed by giving estrogens, if necessary. If local hormonal treatment is used, the remainder of the body's organs will not be greatly affected by the estrogens.

Sometimes a stretching of the bladder opening can help al-leviate some of these symptoms. Women should consult their gynecologist or a urologist about these problems.

Cancer in the Elderly

Many elderly women have an intense fear of cancer. Any mass in the vagina, breasts, or abdomen should be looked into by a physician; reassuringly, most will prove to be benign. Fear of find-ing out what is wrong, however, may delay diagnosis in some pa-tients and turn what would be a simple cure into a complicated problem. No elderly person should ignore symptoms that, at an earlier age, would have made her see her physician. Cancer of the vulva is more common at this age—any unusual sore or lesion should be checked immediately.

Sexual Problems in the Elderly

With age, all body systems undergo change, but none ceases to function completely, and this is true of the sexual organs as well. Specific physiological changes in the functioning of the sexual organs occur with age, due to decreasing strength, tone, and elasticity of the tissues. In addition, an older person will lose an ability that she or he does not use. This applies to sexual functioning just as it applies to walking. Understanding the normal changes that occur in sexual function can help people avoid some of the psychological complications that usually accompany these changes.

Sexual changes in men. It takes an older man a little longer to obtain an erection, and it may also take him a little longer to ejaculate. If a woman accepts this as normal, there is no problem. If the delay is taken as abnormal, two possibilities can occur. The woman may be angry and react in a belittling manner, or she may feel that there is something wrong with her—that her husband no longer finds her attractive.

The erection of an older man will also not be as firm as when he was young, but it will be firm enough for intercourse. Perhaps this is for the better, because the vaginal walls of the older woman are not as elastic either. Both these organs can accommodate the other. Some men get concerned about the diminished quality of their erections. But what is important is a mutually satisfying relationship, not the size of the erection.

Aging men may be unable to ejaculate or sustain an erection.

They may also need more time before obtaining another erection sufficient for intercourse. (However, injections are now available for men to help provide an erection on command.) Another phenomenon is the decrease in the frequency of a man's need to ejaculate. A young man may wish to ejaculate at every opportunity, maybe several times per night, while an older one may want to have—and enjoy—intercourse, yet only ejaculate every third or fourth time. He may not need to ejaculate every time, particularly if the couple is using intercourse as a means of expressing affection and intimacy.

Many women say that they can enjoy sexual intimacy without being orgasmic. Why shouldn't men also enjoy without achieving an orgasm? Some men feel that there may be something wrong with them if they do not ejaculate every time—or perhaps a woman feels that she has not performed well if her husband has not ejaculated. These pressures on both men and women should be avoided. The more pressure a woman puts on a man to achieve an erection or ejaculation, the more trouble he is going to have. A man's sexual pleasure has to be his own, just as a woman's should be her own.

Sexual changes in women. Changes that women experience are not unlike those that occur in their spouse or mate. Response is slower: whereas it takes some young women only thirty seconds of sexual stimulation to become lubricated, in an older woman, vaginal lubrication may take up to five minutes. There may also be a decrease in lubrication with the same amount of stimulation. However, providing a woman is in good health and has continued sexual relations, adequate amounts of lubrication will appear.

Lubrication in women is both a psychological and physiological counterpart of erection in men. Both are probably related to the same neurological and vascular mechanisms. If lubrication appears to be diminished, an artificial lubricant such as Astroglide, Replens, or K-Y jelly may be of value.

Some tranquilizers and some drugs used for high blood pressure can produce a decrease in sexual function. So does alcohol. Sometimes, arthritis interferes with action of the extremities or the hips, so new positions should be explored that might be more comfortable. Some diseases produce fatigue, which diminishes sexual interest and capacity. Chronic fatigue, boredom, depression, hostility, and fear also reduce sexual desire.

Women who remain sexually active do not experience as many vaginal signs of aging as women who discontinue sex. It appears that the skin lining the vagina will remain thicker with use. However, for women with painfully thin vaginal skin, local estrogen and other creams may be prescribed as discussed in chapter 10.

Losing one's spouse or being sexually inactive for a year or two may make it difficult to regain sexual functioning. Masturbation will minimize the difficulty in resuming full sexual functioning, but some elderly women have never masturbated and are concerned that it is not "nice" or acceptable. An understanding physician who explains the anatomical details can be very helpful. Vibrators or devices shaped like a penis may be of value in this regard, depending on individual preference.

Another change that occurs in the elderly woman is that the muscle contractions occurring with orgasm are decreased in strength. However, older women report no decrease in the subjective pleasure or sense of release in sex.

15
Getting Older

The aging process is difficult to assess. Exactly when is one old? Aging actually begins at the moment of birth. Some women are in amazingly good health in both mind and body when they reach their seventies, despite the fact that they may have endured hard work and many stresses throughout their lives. But others deteriorate rapidly.

Heredity and genetics play an important role in determining the rate of aging and longevity. The aging process varies from organ to organ and from person to person. Therefore, in evaluating the problems of elderly people, it is more important to consider the physiological processes of each organ rather than the chronological age itself.

As we age, new problems can arise in various areas of our body. Some are inevitable, but others are preventable—or at least treatable. Here is information to help you understand and care for yourself during the last third of your life.

Eyes and Aging

Poor eyesight is not inevitable with age. Some physical changes occur during the normal aging process that can cause a gradual decline in vision, but most older people maintain good eyesight into their eighties and beyond.

As people get older, they generally need brighter light for such tasks as reading, cooking, or driving a car. In addition, incandescent light bulbs (regular household bulbs) are better than fluorescent lights (tubular overhead lights) for older eyes.

Certain eye disorders and diseases occur more frequently in old age, but a great deal can be done to prevent or correct these conditions.

Here are some suggestions to help protect your eyes:

- Have regular health checkups to detect such treatable diseases as high blood pressure and diabetes, both of which may cause eye problems.
- Have a complete eye examination every two or three years, since many eye diseases have no early noticeable symptoms. The examination should include a vision (and glasses) evaluation, eye muscle check, test for glaucoma, and thorough internal and external eye health exams.
- Seek more frequent eye health care if you have diabetes or a family history of eye disease. Make arrangements for care immediately if you experience signs such as loss or dimness in vision, eye pain, excessive discharge from the eye, double vision, or redness or swelling of the eye or eyelid.

Common Eye Complaints

Presbyopia is a gradual decline in the ability to focus on close objects or to see small print, and is common after the age of forty.

People with this condition often hold reading materials at arm's length, and some may have headaches or "tired eyes" while reading or doing other close work. There is no way to prevent presbyopia, but the focusing problem can be easily compensated for with glasses or contact lenses.

Floaters are tiny spots or specks that float across the field of vision. Most people notice them in well-lighted rooms or outdoors on a bright day. Although floaters are normal and are usually harmless, they may be a warning sign of certain eye problems, such as retinal disorders, especially if associated with light flashes. If you notice a sudden change in the type or number of spots or flashes, call your doctor.

Dry eyes occur when the tear glands produce too few tears. The result is itching, burning, or even reduced vision. An eye specialist can prescribe special eyedrop solutions ("artificial tears") to correct the problem.

Excessive tears may be a sign of increased sensitivity to light, wind, or temperature changes. If so, protective measures such as sunglasses may solve the problem. But tearing may also indicate more serious problems, such as an eye infection or a blocked tear duct, both of which can be treated and corrected.

Common Eye Diseases Associated with Aging

Cataracts are cloudy or opaque areas in part or all of the transparent lens located inside the eye. Normally, the lens is clear and allows light to pass through. When a cataract forms, light cannot easily pass through the lens, and vision is impaired. Cataracts usually develop gradually, without pain, redness, or tearing in the eye. Some remain small and do not seriously affect vision. If a cataract becomes larger or denser, however, the clouded lens can be surgically removed. After surgery, vision is restored with special eyeglasses or contact lenses, or by the insertion of an intraocular lens implant (a plastic lens that is implanted in the eye during surgery). Cataract surgery is a safe procedure that is almost always successful. Still, potential risks and benefits of this elective procedure should be discussed with a doctor.

Glaucoma occurs when there is too much fluid pressure in the eye, causing internal eye damage and gradually destroying vision. The underlying cause of glaucoma is not known, but with early diagnosis and treatment, it can usually be controlled, and blindness prevented. Possible treatments include special eyedrops, oral medications, laser treatments, or in some cases surgery. Glaucoma seldom produces early symptoms, and increased pressure seldom produces pain. For these reasons, it is important for eye specialists to test for the disease during routine eye examinations in those over thirty-five.

Retinal disorders are the leading cause of blindness in the United States. The retina is a thin lining on the back of the eye made up of nerves that receive visual images and pass them on to the brain. Retinal disorders include senile macular degeneration, diabetic retinopathy, and retinal detachment.

Senile macular degeneration is a condition in which the *macula*, the part of the retina responsible for sharp central and reading vision, loses its ability to function efficiently. The first signs may include blurring of reading matter, distortion or loss of central vision (for example, a dark spot in the center of the field of vision), and distortion in vertical lines. Early detection of macular degeneration is important, since some cases may be corrected with laser treatments.

Diabetic retinopathy, one of the possible complications of diabetes, occurs when small blood vessels that nourish the retina fail to do so properly. In the early stages of the condition, the blood vessels may leak fluid, which distorts vision. In the later stages, new vessels may grow and release blood into the center of the eye, resulting in serious loss of vision.

Retinal detachment is a separation between the inner and outer layers of the retina. Detached retinas can usually be surgically reattached with good or partial restoration of vision. New surgical and laser treatments are being used today with increasing success.

Low Vision Aids

Many people with visual impairments can be helped by using low vision aids. These are special devices that provide more power than regular eyeglasses. Low vision aids include telescopic glasses, light-filtering lenses, and magnifying glasses, along with a variety of electronic devices. Some are designed to be hand held; others rest directly on reading material. Partially sighted individuals often notice surprising improvements with the use of these aids.

Teeth and Aging

All too often, older people—especially those who wear dentures— feel they no longer need dental checkups. The idea of preventive dental care dates back only to the 1950s, so most people now over sixty-five were not trained at an early age to be concerned with preventive care of the teeth.

The most important part of good dental care is knowing how to clean your teeth. Brush them on all sides with short strokes, using a soft-bristle brush and any brushing stroke that is comfortable. Pay special attention to the gum line. Brushing your tongue and the roof of your mouth will help remove germs and prevent bad breath. It is best to brush after every meal, but brushing thoroughly at least twice a day, especially at bedtime, is a must. See your dentist if brushing results in repeated bleeding or pain.

Some people with arthritis or other conditions that limit motion may find it hard to hold a toothbrush. If you experience this problem, you can try attaching the brush handle to your hand with a wide elastic band, or enlarge the handle by attaching it to a sponge, styrofoam ball, or similar object. Those with limited shoulder movement might find brushing easier if the handle of the brush is lengthened by attaching a long piece of wood or plastic. Electric toothbrushes can help, too.

Careful daily brushing can help remove plaque, a sticky, colorless film that forms on the teeth and contains harmful germs. If the plaque is not removed every day, it hardens into calculus (tartar), a substance that can be removed only by a dentist or dental hygienist. The buildup of plaque and calculus can lead to periodontal (gum) disease, in which the normally pink gums begin to redden, swell, and occasionally bleed.

If left untreated, periodontal disease will get worse, and pockets of infection will form between the teeth and gums. As the infection spreads, the gums recede. Eventually, the structures that hold the teeth in place are destroyed, the bone socket enlarges, and the tooth loosens and is lost. A regular program of complete oral hygiene can prevent gum disease and tooth decay in most people.

Even though brushing is the most important means of removing film and food particles from the mouth, there are many places a toothbrush cannot reach. To remove germs and pieces of food from between the teeth and near the gum line, dentists recommend daily flossing with dental floss. A dentist or dental hygienist can instruct you in its proper use.

Dentures

When someone loses their teeth because of gum disease or other dental problems, artificial teeth, or dentures, are often prescribed. If you have or get dentures, you should keep them clean and free from deposits that can cause permanent staining, bad breath, and gum irritation. Once a day, brush all surfaces of the dentures with a denture-care product. Remove your dentures from your mouth for at least six hours each day and place them in water (but never in hot water) or a denture-cleansing solution. It is also helpful to rinse your mouth with a warm salt-water solution in the morning, after meals, and at bedtime.

Partial dentures should be cared for in the same way as full dentures. Because germs tend to collect under the clasps of partial dentures, it is especially important that this area be cleaned thoroughly.

Dentures seem awkward at first. When learning to eat with dentures, you should select soft, nonsticky food. Cut food into small pieces, and chew slowly using both sides of the mouth. Dentures tend to make your mouth less sensitive to hot foods and liquids, and less able to detect the presence of harmful objects such as bones. If problems in eating, talking, or simply wearing dentures continue after the first few weeks, your dentist can make proper adjustments.

After a number of years, dentures might have to be realigned, or even replaced. Do not attempt to repair dentures at home, as this can damage the dentures and be harmful to the tissues of the mouth.

Even with good home oral hygiene, it is important to have yearly dental checkups. Many dentists give regular fluoride treatments to adult patients to prevent tooth decay. Dental check-ups not only help maintain a healthy mouth, but are necessary for the early discovery of oral cancer and other diseases. Mouth cancer often goes unnoticed in its early and curable stages, in part because many older people do not visit the dentist often enough, and in part because pain is not an early symptom of the disease. If you notice any red or white spots, or sores in your mouth that bleed or do not go away within two weeks, be sure to have them checked by a dentist.

Taking care of dental problems before undergoing major surgery is essential. The results of a complicated and successful heart operation, for example, could be endangered if certain bacteria that are always present in the mouth get into the bloodstream because of dental disease and lodge on heart valves.

Constipation

Constipation is a symptom, not a disease. It is defined as a decrease in the frequency of bowel movements, accompanied by prolonged or difficult passage of stools. There is no accepted or correct number of daily or weekly bowel movements. Regularity may be a twice-daily bowel movement for some, or two bowel movements a week for others.

Older people are five times as likely as younger people to experience constipation. But experts agree that too often, older people become overly concerned with having a daily bowel movement, and that constipation is frequently an overemphasized ailment.

Some doctors suggest asking yourself these questions to determine if you are really constipated. Do you often have fewer than two bowel movements each week? Do you have difficulty passing stools? Is there pain? Are there other problems such as

218 The Menopause Book

bleeding? Unless these are regular symptoms for you, you are probably not constipated.

Doctors do not always know what causes constipation. It can afflict any older person who eats a poor diet, drinks too few fluids, or misuses laxatives. Drugs used to treat other conditions (certain antidepressants, antacids containing aluminum or calcium, antihistamines, diuretics, and antiparkinsonism drugs) can produce constipation in some patients, as can lack of exercise. Lengthy bed rest after an accident or illness, for example, may contribute to constipation. For patients who stay in bed and who suffer from chronic constipation, drug therapy may be the best solution. But simply being more active is a better idea for individuals who are not bedfast.

A shift in dietary habits away from high-fiber vegetables, fruits, and whole grains to low-fiber foods that are high in animal fats and refined sugars can also lead to constipation. (Some studies have suggested that high-fiber diets result in larger stools and more frequent bowel movements, and therefore less constipation.) Lack of interest in eating—a common problem for many people who live alone—may lead to heavy use of convenience foods, which tend to be low in fiber. In addition, loss of teeth may force older people to choose soft, processed foods that also contain little, if any, fiber.

Older people sometimes cut back on liquids in their diet, especially if they are not eating regular or balanced meals. Water and other fluids add bulk to stools, making bowel movements easier. Ignoring the natural urge to defecate (have a bowel movement) can also result in constipation. Some people prefer to have their bowel movements only at home, but holding a bowel movement can cause ill effects if the delay is too long.

In some people, constipation may be caused by abnormalities or blockage of the digestive system. These disorders may affect either the muscles or nerves responsible for normal defecation. A doctor can perform a series of tests to determine if constipation is the symptom of an underlying (and often treatable) disorder.

Laxatives and Enemas

Americans spend approximately $250 million on over-the-counter (nonprescription) laxatives each year. Many people view them as the cure for constipation. But heavy use of laxatives is usually not necessary and can often be habit-forming. If the body begins to rely on the laxatives to bring on bowel movements, over time, the natural "emptying" mechanisms can fail to work without the help of these drugs. For the same reason, habitual use of enemas can also lead to a loss of normal bowel function. (Conversely, heavy laxative use can also lead to diarrhea.)

Overuse of mineral oil—a popular laxative—may also reduce the absorption of certain vitamins (A,D,E, and K). Mineral oil may also interact with drugs such as anticoagulants (given to prevent blood clots) and other laxatives, causing undesired side effects.

Treatment

If you are constipated, there are steps you can take to improve your condition without resorting to harsh drug treatments. But first, see your doctor to rule out a more serious problem. If the results show that no intestinal disease or other abnormality exists, and your doctor approves, try these remedies:

- Eat more fresh fruits and vegetables, either cooked or raw, as well as more whole-grain cereals and breads. Dried fruits such as apricots, prunes, and figs are especially high in fiber. Try to cut back on highly processed foods, such as sweets, and food high in fat.

- Drink plenty of liquids (1 to 2 quarts daily) unless you have heart, circulatory, or kidney problems. But be aware that some people become constipated from drinking large quantities of milk.

- Some doctors recommend adding small amounts of unprocessed bran ("miller's bran") to baked goods, cereals, and fruits as a way of increasing the fiber content of the diet. If your diet is well-balanced and contains a variety of foods high in natural fiber, it is usually not necessary to add bran to other foods. But if you do use unprocessed bran, remember that some people suffer from bloating and gas for several weeks after adding bran to their diet. All changes in the diet should be made slowly, to allow the digestive system to adapt.

- Stay active. Even taking a brisk walk after dinner can help tone your muscles.

- Try to develop a regular bowel habit. If you have had problems with constipation, attempt to have a bowel movement shortly after breakfast or dinner.

- Avoid taking laxatives if at all possible. Although they will usually relieve the constipation, you can quickly come to depend on them, and the natural muscle actions required for defecation will be impaired.

- Limit your intake of antacids, as some can cause constipation as well as other health problems.

- Above all, do not expect to have a bowel movement every day or even every other day. Regularity differs from person to person. If your bowel movements are usually painless and occur regularly (whether the pattern is three times a day or two times each week), then you are probably not constipated.

Confusion and Memory Loss

Many people are afraid that growing old means losing the ability to think, reason, or remember. They worry when they feel confused or forgetful that these feelings are the first signs of senility. But senility is not an inevitable part of aging. It is true that in the past, doctors did dismiss memory loss, confusion, or similar behaviors as a normal symptom of old age. However, scientists have now found that most old people remain alert and capable until the end of their lives. They know that people who experience changes in their personality, behavior, or mental skills may be suffering from a form of brain disease called dementia.

The term *dementia* is used to describe a group of symptoms that are usually caused by changes in the normal activity of very sensitive brain cells. Dementia seriously interferes with a person's ability to carry out daily activities. Dementia is irreversible: it cannot be cured. However, there are many conditions with symptoms that mimic dementia. These reversible conditions can be caused by problems such as a high fever, poor nutrition, a bad reaction to a medicine, or a minor head injury. Although not dementia, medical problems like these can be serious and should be treated by a doctor as soon as possible.

Sometimes older people have emotional problems that are mistaken for dementia. Feeling sad, lonely, anxious, or bored may be more common for older people facing retirement or handling the death of a relative or friend. Adapting to these changes can leave some people feeling confused or forgetful. Support from friends and relatives or professional counseling can help ease emotional problems.

Check It Out

If you think you might have a form of dementia, you should have a thorough physical, neurological, and psychiatric evaluation. Such an evaluation would include a complete medical exam, as well as tests of your mental abilities. Some tests, such as a brain scan, can help the doctor rule out a curable disorder. Such a scan may also show signs of normal age-related changes in the brain. It may be necessary to repeat the scan at a later date to assess whether changes are taking place at a faster than normal rate.

During a complete medical exam, your physician will also ask you about your medical history, your use of prescription and over-the-counter drugs, your diet, and your general health. Because a correct diagnosis depends on your recalling these details accurately, the doctor may also ask one of your close relatives for information.

The two most common forms of dementia are *vascular dementia* (sometimes called multi-infarct dementia) and *Alzheimer's disease*. In vascular dementia, changes in the brain's blood vessels result in widespread death of brain tissue. Symptoms that begin suddenly may be a sign of this kind of dementia. Telltale signs of vascular dementia include vision or speech problems, numbness or weakness on one side of the body, or both. People with vascular dementia are likely to show signs of improvement or remain stable for long periods of time, then quickly develop new symptoms. Vascular dementia was once thought to be the cause of many cases of irreversible mental impairment. Doctors now believe that most older people with serious mental problems are actually suffering from Alzheimer's disease.

In Alzheimer's disease, nerve cell changes in certain regions of the brain result in the death of a large number of cells. In contrast to vascular dementia, Alzheimer symptoms begin slowly and become steadily worse. Both forms of dementia can exist together, making it hard for a doctor to diagnose either.

Treatment

If your doctor diagnoses an irreversible disorder, there is still much that can be done to treat your symptoms and help your family to cope. Your family members and friends can help you to maintain your daily routines, physical activities, and social contacts. They should also keep you informed about the details of your life—the time of day, where you live, and what is happening at home or in the world. This may help stop brain activity from failing at a more rapid pace. Memory aids can help in day-to-day living. Some families find that a big calendar, a list of daily plans, notes about simple safety measures, and written directions describing how to use common household items can be very helpful.

Proper diet is important, although special diets or supplements are usually not necessary. Medications are often not needed or helpful; but in some people the careful use of drugs can reduce agitation, anxiety, depression, and insomnia.

Although family and friends can help, a person with vascular dementia or Alzheimer's disease should be under the care of a physician—usually a neurologist, psychiatrist, family doctor, internist, or geriatrician is the primary care doctor. Your physician will watch you closely, treat your physical and emotional problems, and answer the many questions that you and your family may have.

Dementia patients lose their abilities at different rates. Even so, there is enough in common in the experiences of patients and their families—the loneliness, the frustration, the lack of information and resources—to have led to the development of family support groups around the country. One of the largest organizations is the Alzheimer's Association (919 North Michigan Avenue, Chicago, IL 60611; telephone 800-272-3900). The Association has more than 200 chapters across the country; it encourages research, education, and family services on all forms of dementia. The Alzheimer's Disease Education and Referral Center (ADEAR) is a clearinghouse supported by the National Institute on Aging that also provides information about vascular dementia and Alzheimer's disease (P.O. Box 8250, Silver Spring, MD 20907-8250).

Hope for Tomorrow

The development of new medications, as well as certain dietary or life-style changes, may someday help prevent or reverse the damage caused by vascular dementia or Alzheimer's disease. Some doctors believe it is very important for people suffering vascular dementia to try to prevent further damage by controlling high blood pressure, monitoring and treating high blood cholesterol, and not smoking.

Developing interests or hobbies and staying involved in activities that keep the mind and body active are among the best ways to remain sharp and retain your mental abilities as you get older. Careful attention to physical fitness, including a balanced diet, may also go a long way to help you preserve a healthy state of mind. Some physical and mental changes occur with age even in healthy persons, but much pain and suffering can be avoided if older persons, their families, and their doctors realize that dementia is a disease, not a normal part of aging.

Urinary Incontinence

Loss of urine control, or *urinary incontinence*, occurs in people of all ages, but is particularly common among older people. At least one in ten persons age sixty-five or older suffers from incontinence. This condition can range from the discomfort of slight losses of urine to the disability and shame of severe, frequent wetting.

Many people with incontinence withdraw from social life and try to hide the problem from their families, friends, and even their doctor. Family members who care for an older person with incontinence often do not know about treatment choices and may believe that nursing-home care is the only option.

These reactions are unfortunate, because in most cases, incontinence can be treated and controlled, if not cured. Incontinence is not an inevitable result of aging. It is caused by specific changes in body function that often stem from diseases or use of medications. Incontinence may be brought on by an illness that causes fatigue and confusion, or one requiring a hospital admission. Incontinence is sometimes the first and only symptom of a urinary tract infection. Curing the illness usually will relieve or clear up the incontinence.

If you have problems controlling urination, you should see your doctor. Even when incontinence cannot be completely cured, modern products and ways of managing the condition can ease the discomfort and inconvenience it causes.

Types of Incontinence

The following are the most common types of urinary incontinence:

Stress incontinence is the leakage of urine during exercise, coughing, sneezing, laughing, lifting heavy objects, or other body movements that put pressure on the bladder. It is the most common type of incontinence and can almost always be cured (see chapter 14).

Urge incontinence is the inability to hold urine long enough to reach a toilet. It is often found in people who suffer from diabetes, stroke, dementia, Parkinson's disease, and multiple sclerosis. It can also be a warning sign of early bladder cancer. (In men, it is often a sign of an enlarged prostate.) It can, however, occur in otherwise healthy older persons.

Overflow incontinence is the leakage of small amounts of urine from a bladder that is always full. (In older men, this can occur when the flow of urine from the bladder is blocked.) One cause of an overfull bladder is loss of normal bladder contractions in some people with diabetes.

Functional incontinence occurs in many older people who have normal urine control but who have difficulty reaching a toilet in time because of arthritis or other crippling disorders.

Diagnosis

Diagnosis generally involves giving a detailed history of health and related problems, as well as undergoing a physical examination that focuses on the urinary tract, nervous system, and reproductive organs. The doctor will probably also want to check a urine sample. In many cases, the patient will then be referred to a urologist, a doctor who specializes in diseases of the urinary tract.

Treatment

Treatment of urinary incontinence should be tailored to each patient's needs. As a general rule, the least dangerous procedures should be tried first. The many options include the following:

- Certain behavioral techniques—including pelvic muscle exercises, biofeedback, and bladder training—are helpful in controlling urination. These techniques can help a person sense the bladder filling and delay voiding until he or she can reach a toilet.
- A number of medications can be used to treat incontinence. However, these drugs may cause side effects such as a dry mouth, eye problems, and buildup of urine; therefore, they must be used carefully under a doctor's supervision.
- Several types of surgery can improve or even cure incontinence that is related to a structural problem such as an abnormally positioned bladder. Devices that replace or aid the muscles controlling urine flow are also available; many of these devices require surgical implantation.

Management

Sometimes incontinence cannot be cured, but it can be managed. Specially designed absorbent underclothing is available. Many of these garments are no more bulky than normal underwear and can be worn easily under everyday clothing.

Incontinence may also be managed by inserting a flexible tube known as a catheter into the urethra, and collecting the urine in a container. However, long-term catheterization, although sometimes necessary, creates many problems, including urinary infections.

It is important not to let embarrassment discourage a per-

son from seeking a doctor's care—particularly because incontinence can be treated and often cured. Even incurable problems
can be managed to reduce complications, anxiety, and stress.

Diabetes

Diabetes mellitus is a disorder in which the body cannot convert
foods properly into the energy needed for daily activity. When
a person eats sugars and starches, the body usually changes them
into a form of sugar called glucose. Glucose is a type of fuel that
travels through the bloodstream for immediate use by the body's
cells, or is stored in the liver for future use.

In diabetes, the mechanism that controls the amount of
glucose in the blood breaks down. The glucose builds up to dangerous levels, causing symptoms like extreme thirst and frequent
need to urinate, and damaging body organs. This buildup occurs either because the body does not have enough insulin (the
hormone that regulates the glucose level in the blood) or because the insulin is not fully effective on body tissues.

Diabetes tends to run in families, but factors other than
heredity are also associated with the disease. For example, becoming overweight can trigger diabetes in susceptible older people.

There are two main types of diabetes. Type I, or *insulin-
dependent diabetes*, is the more severe form of the disease.
Although this type of diabetes can appear at any age, it generally starts during childhood or adolescence. Lifelong treatment
with insulin is required, along with exercise and a controlled diet.

The most common form of diabetes among older people is
type II, or *non-insulin-dependent diabetes*. Previously known as
"adult-onset" diabetes, this form accounts for over 90 percent
of all cases. Most people with this type of diabetes do not need

insulin injections. They can usually keep their blood glucose levels near normal by controlling their weight, exercising, and following a sensible diet.

Blood glucose levels that are either very high or very low can lead to serious medical emergencies. Diabetics may go into a coma when their blood sugar levels get very high. Low blood sugar can also lead to unconsciousness. People who have diabetes must know the warning signs and what to do if problems occur. In addition, the disease can lead to serious long-term complications, which include stroke, blindness, heart disease, kidney failure, gangrene, and nerve damage. Proper blood glucose control will help prevent or lessen these problems.

Detecting Diabetes

Sometimes, the first sign of diabetes is found by a doctor. He or she may detect some sugar in the urine or too much sugar in the blood during a routine test. In other cases, the problem is uncovered by a glucose tolerance test. This test measures the level of glucose in the blood before, and at timed intervals after, drinking a special liquid. Research shows that elevation in blood glucose levels often occurs with age, though the increase is usually a result of added body weight, particularly when excess fat accumulates around the waist.

Some people with diabetes feel "run down" or have vague symptoms that may go unrecognized. Others have symptoms such as increased thirst, frequent urination, unexplained weight loss, fatigue, blurred vision, skin infections or itching, and slow-healing cuts and bruises. Any of these problems should be reported promptly to a doctor.

Treatment

Diabetes cannot be cured, but it can be controlled. Good control requires a careful blend of diet, exercise, and possibly insulin injections or oral medications.

Diet is crucial to lowering blood glucose levels. In planning a diet, the doctor considers the patient's weight, as well as the amount of physical activity the patient engages in each day. For overweight patients, a weight-reducing plan is essential to achieve proper blood glucose control. Food–exchange lists to help with meal planning are available from physicians and from the American Diabetes Association (1660 Duke Street, Alexandria, VA 22314; telephone–800-232-3472).

Exercise is also important because it helps the body burn off some of the excess glucose as energy. Studies have shown that engaging in a regular fitness program reduces blood glucose in older people who have elevated levels, including those with diabetes. A doctor can help plan an exercise program that takes into account your diet, medication needs, and general health. It is important to be consistent, exercising about the same amount each day. This will prevent injury and lower your baseline heart rate.

Drugs are not needed for non-insulin-dependent diabetes if good control can be achieved through diet and exercise. But when these measures fail, insulin injections or oral drugs may be prescribed. Sometimes, a patient who normally does well without drugs will need to take medication for a short time during acute illnesses.

Foot care is essential for people with diabetes, because the disease can cut down the blood supply to the feet and reduce sensation in these extremities. If you have diabetes, you should examine your feet every day, taking note of any redness or patches of heat. Any sores, blisters, breaks in the skin, infections, or buildup of calluses should be reported immediately to a podiatrist or family doctor.

Skin care in other parts of the body is also very important. People with diabetes are less able than others to resist injury and infection. They need to protect their skin against injury, keep it clean, use skin softeners to treat dryness, and take care of minor cuts and bruises.

Teeth and gums must also receive special attention to avoid serious infections. If you have diabetes, inform your dentist of your condition and see him or her regularly.

In general, diabetes is a self-help disease. If a diabetic sticks to a diet plan, exercises regularly, takes prescribed medication, and observes good health practices, she can enjoy a healthy and productive life.

Arthritis

The term *arthritis* means inflammation of a joint. The disease commonly known as arthritis (also called *rheumatic disease*) actually encompasses many different conditions, which vary in symptoms and probably in cause. Some forms are better understood than others, but the causes of most of them are not yet known. Many effective treatments are used today to control arthritic symptoms, but there are few cures.

Most forms of arthritis are usually chronic, lasting for years. The most serious forms involve inflammation (swelling, warmth, redness, and pain). The two most comon forms of arthritis in older women are rheumatoid arthritis and osteoarthritis.

Rheumatoid arthritis is an inflammation of the joint membrane. It varies in severity and can cause severe crippling. Rheumatoid arthritis afflicts three times more women than men, and usually appears in the middle years, though it can begin at any age.

Rheumatoid arthritis can affect many body systems, but most frequently appears in the joints—fingers, wrists, elbows, hips, knees, and ankles. Persistent swelling and pain in joints on both sides of the body are typical symptoms. Morning stiffness is especially common. Rheumatoid arthritis should be treated as soon as it is discovered, because uncontrolled inflammation of joint membranes can damage the joints.

Osteoarthritis is also called *degenerative joint disease,* a more accurate name since the term osteoarthritis implies that inflammation is a part of the disease, which is not usually the case. Although wear and tear on the inside surface of the joint is probably a cause of some cases, heredity and overweight may be other possible factors.

Osteoarthritis is often a mild condition, causing no symptoms in many people and only occasional joint pain and stiffness in others. Still, some people experience considerable pain and disability. Though most elderly people have some degree of osteoarthritis, the condition can occur at any age, especially after a joint injury. Joint stiffness in osteoarthritis can be brief, is often relieved by activity, and may recur upon rest. The large weight-bearing joints of the body—knees, hips, and spine—are most often affected.

Treatment

The aim in treating arthritis is to relieve pain and stiffness, stop joint destruction from inflammation, and maintain mobility.

Aspirin relieves pain and reduces joint inflammation, and is the medicine most frequently used to treat arthritis. ("Arthritis-strength" aspirins are plain aspirin with small amounts of caffeine or antacids.) But aspirin should be taken for arthritis only under medical supervision since large doses are required to reduce inflammation. In addition, long-term use of aspirin can cause stomach irritation or other side effects, and may interfere with blood clotting.

Acetaminophen is a common aspirin substitute that does not reduce inflammation, although it can relieve aches and pains. Newer drugs used instead of aspirin are nonsteroidal and anti-inflammatory drugs (NSAIDs). These include ibuprofen, naproxen, fenoprofen, tolmetin, and sulindac. They are similar to aspirin in their ability to reduce inflammation, but may have fewer side effects. Indomethacin, oxyphenbutazone, and phenylbutazone are other NSAIDs that provide relief for patients with arthritis, but they may have more side effects. At this time, one of the newest NSAIDs, piroxicam, offers the advantage of a once-daily dosage.

Other stronger or nonaspirin drugs available by prescription include antimalarial drugs (such as hydroxychloroquine), gold salts, steroids (including prednisone and cortisone), and penicillamine (not the same as penicillin). These drugs tend to have more serious side effects than aspirin, however.

Physical therapy is fundamental to treatment. People with arthritis tend not to move around very much, and while some rest can reduce inflammation, too much stiffens joints. Rest and exercise must be balanced. Daily exercise like walking or swimming can help maintain joint mobility. Good posture and proper eating (to prevent overweight) can help relieve joint strain.

Surgery is sometimes used in patients with rheumatoid arthritis or osteoarthritis when joints are severely damaged and the most conservative forms of treatment have failed to control pain. Hip and knee joints are replaced most often. The purpose of surgery is to relieve pain and restore joint function to patients who have not had any success with other forms of treatment.

Unproven and "Quack" Cures

Arthritic symptoms, especially those associated with rheumatoid arthritis, may go away by themselves, but often reappear weeks, months, or years later. This sudden disappearance of symptoms makes arthritis an ideal target for quack products or gimmicks. Some of the more common are the following:

DMSO (dimethyl sulfoxide). Currently, this drug is approved only for the treatment of interstitial cystitis, a bladder disorder. Studies are now being conducted to determine the safety and effectiveness of DMSO for the treatment of certain other illnesses, but as yet, there is no evidence that it is useful for arthritis.

Special diet. Diet is not a factor in the cause or treatment of arthritis. Any ads promoting certain foods, vitamins, or diets as cures are misleading.

Medical devices. Magnetic bandages, vibrators, or other gadgets are of no use in treating arthritis. Be wary of ads that use words such as "cure" or "miracle treatment."

Warning Signs of Arthritis

Any recurring joint symptoms lasting longer than six weeks should be checked with your doctor, no matter how mild or "temporary." A physical examination, X-ray studies, and specific laboratory tests can distinguish arthritis from other ailments, and can pinpoint the specific type of arthritis that is responsible for your symptoms.

Important arthritis warning signs are these:

- Pain, tenderness, or swelling in one or more joints
- Pain and stiffness in the morning
- Recurring or persistent pain and stiffness in the neck, lower back, or knees
- Symptoms that go away for a week or a month, but then return

Cancer in Older People

The chances of surviving cancer today are better than ever before. But tumors are more likely to be treated successfully when they are detected early. You can help safeguard your health by learning the early warning signs of cancer and having regular checkups.

Most people know something about cancer, but fear keeps many of them from finding out what they can do about it. Because many cancers occur most often in people ages fifty and older, it is this age group that has the most to gain from learning about symptoms of the disease.

Early Warning Signs

The following are early warning signs for the most common cancers to strike postmenopausal women:

- Lung: A cough that won't go away; coughing up blood; shortness of breath.
- Breast: A lump in the breast; a change in breast shape; discharge from the nipple.
- Colon or rectal: Changes in bowel habits; bleeding from the rectum; blood in the stool, which appears bright red or black.
- Uterus, ovary, and cervix: Bleeding after menopause; unusual vaginal discharge; enlargement of the abdomen; pain during intercourse.
- Skin: A sore that does not heal; a change in the shape, size, or color of a wart or mole; the sudden appearance of a mole.

If you have any of these symptoms, contact your doctor as soon as possible to find out if an office visit is necessary. Your symptoms may point to an illness other than cancer. Remember, pain is usually not an early warning sign of cancer.

Some people, as they age, attribute medical symptoms to "growing older." Because of this, many illnesses go untreated. Do not fail to mention symptoms to your doctor just because you think they are unimportant or normal for your age. Also, feel free to ask your doctor questions and press for further explanation if you don't understand his or her responses. You might try listing your questions before an office visit—take time to record your doctor's answers as well.

Regular Checkups

Even if you do not have symptoms, there are certain tests you should undergo periodically once you reach fifty. Some women ought to get certain tests even earlier. Your doctor can tell you how often you should have specific tests, based on your medical history and generally accepted guidelines. Some may be required more often if you have had cancer before, have a family member with cancer, or have other medical conditions.

Guaiac test. One or more small stool samples are examined for possible traces of blood. Blood in the stool can be a symptom of colon or rectal cancer. There are simple kits available for the collection of samples at home; samples can then be mailed or delivered to the doctor's office.

Rectal exam. An examination of the rectum with the doctor's gloved finger can detect rectal tumors.

Sigmoidoscopy (or "procto"). A long, narrow, flexible instrument with a lighted scope on the end is inserted into the rectum to check the rectum and part of the colon for traces of colon or rectal cancer. Unlike the Guaiac test, this examination can identify precancerous changes or growths (polyps) that would alert your physician to observe you more closely.

Pelvic examination and Pap test. These tests are routine for most women by the time they reach menopause. The pelvic exam is a check of the female reproductive organs. The doctor, using gloved fingers and a small instrument called a speculum, checks the vagina, uterus, and ovaries for any sign of a problem. A Pap test, also called a Pap smear, is usually done at the same time. It is a painless test that involves removing cells from the cervix and examining them through a microscope to see if they are abnormal.

Breast examination and mammography. Women should have their breasts examined periodically to check for changes such as a lump or thickening (see chapter 13). A mammogram can detect tumors even before they can be felt. Check that the equipment used for mammography exposes you to the lowest possible dose of radiation. Generally, the amount should be less than 1 rad (a measure of radiation dose) for each breast. In addition to tests performed by a doctor, women should practice breast self-examination (BSE) monthly to detect lumps or other changes in their breasts.

A positive result on any of these medical tests does not necessarily mean you have cancer, but it may indicate a need for more testing. If a tumor is suspected, a biopsy is required. A piece of the tumor is removed surgically and examined microscopically to determine whether it is cancerous (malignant) or noncancerous (benign).

What If the Doctor Diagnoses Cancer?

If tests show that you have cancer, you should begin treatment right away. Cancer is a disease in which cells grow abnormally. If left untreated, the cells continue to grow and eventually invade healthy tissue.

A number of treatments may be used for cancer. To ensure that you will be comfortable with your decision to have a particular treatment, you may want to seek the opinion of more than one doctor. Ask your doctor if you should see an oncologist (a cancer specialist). The National Cancer Institute has specialty panels made up of experts on various types of cancer who can evaluate your medical records and suggest a course of treatment. (Their toll-free telephone number is 800-4-CANCER.) It is important to ask questions about your diagnosis and the results that are expected from treatment.

Remember that a diagnosis of cancer is not a death sentence. When found early—and taken care of as quickly as possible—many cancers today are curable.

16
Conclusion

The generation of women now in their perimenopausal years is the same group who, when entering their childbearing years a few decades ago, asked for and received information about their bodies and their health. These women—the so-called baby boomers—revolutionized obstetrical care by insisting on knowledge and participation. They have come to expect that they will be informed and take part in all of their health care decisions. This more-educated generation derives security from knowledge, rather than from mystique and paternalism.

We have attempted in this book to provide the information necessary to expose the myths and misinformation concerning menopause. We have tried to present the facts as they are currently understood. However, this is a rapidly changing field. Your education must continue in a partnership with your physician. This education will make you a participant, rather than a victim, of your health care.

We have tried to give you a general picture of what to expect, and how to enjoy—and thrive in—what we consider to be just another phase of a long and healthy life. Menopause is just the beginning of the last third of life. It is not a disease: perhaps you will need hormone replacement therapy, and perhaps you will not. What is important is that you make the decision in conjunction with your physician in an enlightened and fearless manner.

Menopause can be a time to create a new lifestyle, one that is productive and fulfilling. Knowledge and lack of trepidation will help you achieve this.

Good luck, and good health!

Index

About the Authors

Sheldon H. Cherry, M.D., is a clinical professor of obstetrics and gynecology at the Mount Sinai School of Medicine in New York City, where he is also in private practice. His previous books include *Understanding Pregnancy and Childbirth*, *The Menopause Myth*, *Planning Ahead for Pregnancy*, and *For Women of All Ages*. Carolyn D. Runowicz, M.D., is the director of the Division of Gynecologic Oncology and associate professor of obstetrics and gynecology at the Albert Einstein College of Medicine, Bronx, New York.

The authors, both prominent physicians, represent a combined experience of more than forty years in gynecology and women's health. Between them they have published more than eighty papers in their fields. They are, incidentally, husband and wife.